A HIKING GUIDE TO NEW BRUNSWICK

A Hiking Guide to NEW BRUNSWICK

Marianne and H.A. Eiselt

GOOSE LANE

Published by Goose Lane Editions with the assistance of the New Brunswick Department of Municipalities, Culture and Housing and the Department of Canadian Heritage, 1996.

Cover photograph by Brian Atkinson, 1995. Reproduced with permission of the Artist. Back cover photograph taken by H.A. Eiselt at Mount Douglas Bald (fall 1995).
Book design and maps by Brenda Berry.
Edited by Charles Stuart and Laurel Boone.
Printed and bound in Canada by Tribune Printing.

10   9   8   7   6   5   4   3   2

Canadian Cataloguing in Publication Data
    Eiselt, Marianne.
    A hiking guide to New Brunswick

    Includes bibliographical references and index.
    ISBN 0-86492-188-8

1. Trails — New Brunswick — Guidebooks.
2.Hiking — New Brunswick — Guidebooks.
3. New Brunswick — Guidebooks.
I. Eiselt, Horst A., 1950- .   II. Title.

GV199.44.C22N46 1996   917.15'1044   C96 950030-0

Goose Lane Editions
469 King Street
Fredericton, New Brunswick
CANADA E3B 1E5

If you want inner peace, find it in solitude, not speed. And, if you would find yourself, look to the land from which you came and to which you go.
— Henry David Thoreau

Herring weir, Grand Manan. H.A. EISELT

CONTENTS

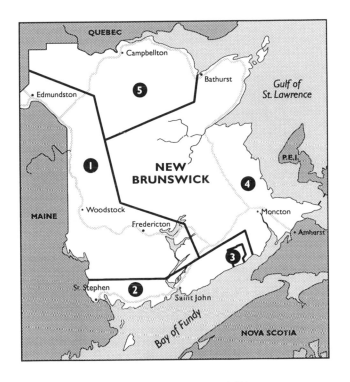

1. ST. JOHN RIVER VALLEY
2. FUNDY COAST
3. FUNDY NATIONAL PARK
4. EASTERN SHORES
5. APPALACHIAN HIGHLANDS

Trail Name	Difficulty	km (mi)
ST. JOHN RIVER VALLEY		
Second Falls Nature Trail	e	4.2 (2.6)
Hays Falls Trail	e	3.4 (2.1)
Lookout Nature Trail	e	0.6 (0.4)
Streamside Nature Trail	e	1.8 (1.1)
Nackawic Nature Trail	e	3.2 (2.0)
Boulderwalk Trail	e	4.8 (3.0)
MACTAQUAC PROVINCIAL PARK Beaver Pond Trail	e	5.0 (3.0)
Alex Creek Trail	e	2.2 (1.4)
Maple Sugar Trail	e	1.8 (1.1)
Jones Field – Marina Trail	e-m	3.2 (2.0)
Odell Park Loop	e-m	5.2 (3.2)
Mount Douglas Bald Trail	m	2.5 (1.6)
Turtle Mountain Trail	m	20.8 (13.0) + 3.2 (2.0)

e = easy   e-m = easy to moderate   m = moderate
m-s = moderate to strenuous   s = strenuous

Trail Name	Difficulty	km (mi)
FUNDY COAST		
ROOSEVELT CAMPOBELLO INTERNATIONAL PARK & HERRING COVE PROVINCIAL PARK Roosevelt Cottage Loop Trail	e-m	7.2 (4.5) + 3.3 (2.0)
Upper Duck Pond Trail	e	5.0 (3.1)
Lower Duck Pond Trail	e-m	6.0 (3.7)
GRAND MANAN ISLAND Lighthouse Trail	m	36.4 (22.6) one way
Money Cove Loop	m	13.8 (8.6)
Eel Lake Trail	m	7.2 (4.4)
Flock of Sheep Trail	e-m	6.0 (3.8)
Red Point Trail	e	3.0 (1.9)
Beech Hill	e	1.0 (0.6)
Sunbury Shores Nature Trail	e	0.8 (0.5)
New River Beach Trail	e	5.0 (3.1)
Taylor Island Perimeter Trail	e	6.3 (4.0)
Sheldon Point Trail	e-m	8.0 (5.0)
Rockwood Park Loop	e-m	8.6 (5.3)
Hammond River Nature Trail	e-m	1.7 (1.1)
Fundy Footpath	s	25.7 (16.0) one way
FUNDY NATIONAL PARK		
East Branch	e	5.6 (3.5)

A HIKING GUIDE TO NEW BRUNSWICK

Trail Name	Difficulty	km (mi)
Bennett Brook	m-s	15.8 (9.8)
Caribou Plain Trail	e	3.4 (2.1)
Tracey Lake (from Laverty Lake)	e-m	5.6 (3.5)
Tracey Lake (from Bennett Lake)	e	8.2 (5.2)
Coppermine Trail	e	4.4 (2.8)
Goose River Trail	m	15.8 (9.8)
Marven Lake Trail	e-m	16.0 (10.0)
Shiphaven Trail	e	1.0 (0.6)
Foster Brook Trail	m	4.8 (3.8)
Squaws Cap Loop	e-m	4.9 (3.0)
Devils Half Acre	e	1.1 (0.7)
Dickson Falls	e	1.0 (0.6)
Shaded Maples Trail	e	0.5 (0.3)
Coastal Trail	m	20.2 (12.6)
Whitetail Trail	m-s	12.2 (7.6)
Upper Salmon River Trail	m-s	15.8 (10.0)
Black Hole Trail	e-m	11.0 (6.8)
The Forks Trail	m-s	6.8 (4.2)
Moosehorn Trail	m	4.4 (2.8)
Laverty Falls Trail	e-m	5.0 (3.2)
Kinnie Brook Trail	e	2.8 (1.8)
Third Vault Falls Trail	e-m	7.4 (4.6)

Trail Name	Difficulty	km (mi)
EASTERN SHORES		
New Horton Marsh	e	9.0 (5.6)
Shepody National Wildlife Area	e	14.8 (9.2)
Marys Point Peninsula	m	6.5 (4.0)
Cape Maringouin	e	5.2 (3.2)
Westcock Marsh	e	5.3 (3.3)
Sackville Waterfowl Park	e	2.0 (1.2)
Paunchy Lake	e	6.0 (3.7)
Dobson Trail	m	58.4 (36.5) one way
Hayward Pinnacle	m-s	4.2 (2.6)
Centennial Park Loop	e	4.0 (2.5)
Buctouche Sandbar	e-m	22.6 (14.2)
South Richibucto Sandbar	e-m	17.2 (10.8)
Point Escuminac Beach Trail	m	12.4 (7.8)
French Fort Cove	e	6.4 (4.0)
Little Sheephouse Falls Nature Trail	e	0.8 (0.5)
KOUCHIBOUGUAC NATIONAL PARK Tweedie Trail	e	1.2 (0.7)
Osprey Trail	e	5.1 (3.2)
Claire Fontaine Trail	e	3.0 (1.8)
Pines Trail	e	0.8 (0.5)
Beaver Trail	e	1.4 (0.9)

A HIKING GUIDE TO NEW BRUNSWICK

Trail Name	Difficulty	km (mi)
Cedars Trail	e	1.0 (0.6)
Salt Marsh	e	0.8 (0.5)
Kellys Beach Nature Trail	e	1.4 (0.9)
The Bog	e	2.0 (1.2)
La Source Trail	e	2.6 (1.6)
Kouchibouguac River Trail	e-m	16.8 (10.4)
Daly Point Reserve Nature Trail	e	5.0 (3.1)
APPALACHIAN HIGHLANDS		
Big Bald Mountain Trail	m	11.0 (6.8)
Sadlers Nature Trail	e	1.7 (1.1)
Charlo Dam Loop	e-m	6.3 (3.9)
SUGARLOAF PROVINCIAL PARK Sugarloaf Summit Trail	m-s	5.1 (3.2)
Prichard Lake Trail	e-m	12.6 (7.8)
Sugarloaf Big Loop	e-m	18.5 (11.5)
MOUNT CARLETON PROV. PARK Mount Bailey Trail	m	7.5 (4.7) +1.6 (1.0)
Bald Mountain Brook Trail	m-s	5.5 (3.5)
Mount Sagamook Trail	s	8.1 (5.0) + 2.5 (1.6)
Mount Head Trail	m	4.8 (3.0)
Mount Carleton Trail	m	9.8 (6.1) + 2.5 (1.5)

Trail Name	Difficulty	km (mi)
Big Brook – Dry Brook Loop	m-s	19.6 (12.2)
Caribou Brook Trail	e	10.0 (6.2)
Pine Point Trail	e	2.2 (1.4)
Williams Falls	e	0.6 (0.4)

PREFACE TO THE SECOND EDITION

Writing this book was a lot of work, but it was also a pleasure. Our planning was a lot better this time than it was when we wrote the first edition of *A Hiking Guide to New Brunswick*, where we had virtually no mishaps – good, of course, as things went smoothly on the trail; sad, on the other hand, as we were deprived of telling those "I almost-got-lost-but-then-finally-found-the-trail-again" hiking stories to awe-struck tyros. What remains is the pleasant task of thanking all those who were involved in the project in one way or another.

We would like to acknowledge some of the people who helped us in preparing the first edition of this hiking guide. Thanks to forest ranger LeRoy Johnson in Mount Carleton Provincial Park for sharing his thoughts and knowledge about the park along with cups of much-needed coffee. Thanks also to forest ranger Peter Pinder, who gave us a memorable mountain ride in the back of his pickup with his dog, Tyson. We're still scared. Our appreciation goes to an unknown man and his two boys who hauled our (then) brand-new pickup out of the mud. They didn't believe that a grownup man and woman were in the woods on a Sunday evening, shortly before dark, looking for a hiking trail. It does sound silly. Our thanks also to Joan Davis for looking after our four kitties during our absence. Furthermore, we are grateful to Eric Hadley of the Department of Natural Resources for his invaluable information and advice.

We would also like to thank a number of people for their help with the second edition. Some stand out: Edwin Melanson for his guidance, car shuttles, and information about the new Fundy Footpath; Art MacFadden for showing us Turtle Mountain; and forest ranger Patrick MacKinley for sharing his knowledge about Fundy National Park with us. Finally, thanks go out to Heidi Grein and Andy Smith's family for caring for our cats during our absence. Last, but certainly not least, we wish to express our gratitude to Susanne Alexander, Laurel Boone, Julie Scriver, Brenda Berry and Charles Stuart of Goose Lane Editions for their help and co-operation.

INTRODUCTION

Although camping, fishing and boating claim larger numbers, hiking has rapidly increased in popularity in this province over the last two decades. This trend can be measured by the growth of new hiking clubs and the increasing numbers of hikers in national and provincial parks. This is by no means an isolated phenomenon. Many European countries are laced with trails, and the United States boasts a tremendous system, crowned by the Appalachian Trail (from Georgia to Maine) and the Pacific Crest Trail (from Mexico to Canada), each exceeding two thousand miles in length, and the new American Discovery Trail from California to Delaware, which comprises a staggering 4,800 miles. And these trails are used not just by tough and rugged individuals who hike these paths in their entirety, but by "regular" people who might spend only a few hours or days on them.

One reason for the popularity of hiking is that, in its simplest form, it does not require any special equipment. **Walking trails** (less than two hours, easy going) can be attempted by all, including kids, and **hiking trails** (up to a full day) are for reasonably fit individuals. Multi-day **backpacking** trails (two to seven days) attract physically fit nature lovers, and **long-distance backpacking** trails are for those who seriously want to get away from it all. Clearly, multi-day hikes, particularly those over difficult terrain, do require special and sometimes costly gear. In this book, we describe trails that run the gamut from walks to multi-day hikes. There should be a trail for everyone here.

Hiking is not about arriving at a destination; it is about the experience of getting there. Hiking is almost always combined with other pursuits such as bird-watching, photography or the plain enjoyment of the outdoors. Fresh air and fitness are extra bonuses. There are many questions a would-be hiker is likely to ask. In this book, we don't discuss the how's or why's of this activity. This book addresses the questions, Where can I hike in the Province of New Brunswick? and What will I find on these trails?

In order to get a feel for what can be expected on the hiking trails in this province, it is useful to know some basic facts about its geography. New Brunswick's surface is about 28,000 square miles, 85% of which is wooded; and the elevation ranges from sea level to 2,700 feet. Even though most of the province's geologic structure was formed in the paleozoic era, 248–590 million years ago, the surface is astonishingly diverse: it ranges from wide, sandy beaches to highlands to fertile river valleys. In this second edition of *A Hiking Guide to New Brunswick*, we have divided the province into five geographical regions where hiking trails can be found.

The first region is the scenic **St. John River Valley**, a fertile area where agriculture is one of the economic mainstays. It extends from the Madawaska region in the northwest corner of the province through Fredericton to Grand Lake. Along the **Fundy Coast**, life on the Fundy Isles has a slower pace than it does on the mainland. Charming fishing communities, the Franklin D. Roosevelt cottage on Campobello Island and whale-watching, hiking, and ocean kayaking activities on Grand Manan attract local and foreign tourists. The entire Fundy Coast is dominated by the tides; rising to 50 feet, they are among the highest in the world due to the funnel-like shape of the Bay of Fundy. The weather and the tides have formed a dramatic shoreline of jagged cliffs and rocky beaches, and the forest often ends abruptly at the steep cliffs. Forestry, fishing and tourism are the main industries along the Fundy coast. **Fundy National Park** encompasses a diverse landscape: the Bay of Fundy with its giant tides and softwood-clad cliffs, and, in the uplands, roaring waterfalls and large stands of maple, birch and beech. The park is a haven for hikers and naturalists. Just east of Fundy National Park, the geography suddenly changes. The **Eastern Shores** are characterized by fishing villages, lighthouses, marshes, peat bogs and miles of sandy beaches. Salt marshes predominate along the southern end of the Eastern Shores. The dikes and sea walls in this area are splendid examples of how the early Acadian settlers controlled the tremendous tides. The shores of the Northumberland Strait boast miles of sandy beaches with the warmest salt water north of Virginia. The hinterland does, however, change gradually; it is fertile in the south and increasingly barren in the north. Bogs become more and more prevalent north of Kouchibouguac National Park which features sandy beaches, salt marshes and lagoons. Farther north, the Eastern Shores melt into the Bay of Chaleur, where commercial fishing is the mainstay for most Acadian residents. In New Brunswick's centre, the Miramichi River and its many tributaries rule the landscape as they flow through the heavily wooded basin. Going northwest, the land slowly rises towards the **Appalachian Highlands,** the New Brunswick portion of the range that extends from the southeastern United States to Newfoundland. The rounded shape of the heavily wooded highlands suggests advanced geological age. The major feature is Mount Carleton, the highest peak of the Maritimes and the centrepiece of Mount Carleton Provincial Park.

WHAT'S NEW?

The hiking trails that have changed the most in recent years are in the Fundy Isles along the Fundy coast. Kouchibouguac National Park has fewer hiking trails and emphasizes cycling instead.

The Grand Manan trails have undergone the most visible improvements. The "Friends of Grand Manan Trails" have done a super job of keeping the trails open. When we hiked them in the summer of 1995 — after devastating storms during the previous fall — there was virtually no deadfall on the trail. The trails are marked by unambiguous blazing; we have pointed out the very few exceptions. And, for good measure, the Grand Manan trailblazers have made the entire west coast of the island hikeable. We applaud their efforts without reservation.

The newly established Fundy Footpath leads westward from Fundy National Park along the rugged Fundy coast. This is another volunteer project and another excellent achievement. Edwin Melanson and the Moncton Outdoor Enthusiasts, who established and maintain the Dobson Trail, New Brunswick's first multiday hiking trail, have done it again. They have blazed the Fundy Footpath from the end of the Goose River Trail at the southwestern boundary of Fundy National Park for some 26 km (16 mi) along the coast past Martin Head to Dustan Brook near Little Salmon River. A tremendous job and a good trail.

As a commitment to protect the environment, new nature trails have been built by corporations along rivers and the Fundy coast. These include Taylor Island Perimeter Trail and Sheldon Point Trail in the Irving Nature Park on Taylor Island, near Saint John, and the St. Anne Pulp and Paper Company's Lookout Nature Trail and Streamside Nature Trail in Big Pokiok Nature Park on the scenic Pokiok River near Nackawic. Other industry-sponsored trails are the Fraser Company's Second Vault Falls Trail, near Edmundston, and the Miramichi Pulp and Paper Company's Little Sheephouse Falls Nature Trail in the Miramichi Basin.

Kouchibouguac National Park has undergone a transition away from hiking towards beach pleasures, canoeing and cycling. Some trails have been converted to bicycle trails, for instance the Major Kollock Trail. While hiking is not expressly prohibited on these trails, we have not included them in this edition of *A Hiking Guide to New Brunswick*. This development is not necessarily bad; it gives the park a clearer focus. Furthermore, concentrating opportunities for various activities in different parks eliminates having to drive for several hours between one hiking trail and the next.

Lately, there has been a shift in government policy towards favouring multi-use trails. These trails are designed to be shared by various groups of users, such as hikers, bikers and horseback riders in the summer, and cross-country skiers and snowmobilers in the winter. We do not believe that this is a good idea as different groups have very different needs. Whereas cyclists need a sufficiently wide trail with a solid surface, hikers get a much better walk and cause only minimal erosion on a trail with a soil surface. Also, as unpleasant as it is for hikers to be on the alert for cyclists, it is no less irritating for bikers to have to be on a permanent lookout for hikers. As usual, the stronger crowds out the weaker. Furthermore, all the multi-use trails that we have seen are very wide and level — in other words, not very exciting for hiking. For this reason we do not include them in our book.

We have also noticed an increasing tendency to make trails "nice" with long and often unnecessary boardwalk sections through woods. Such overdevelopment is particularly obvious in New River Beach

Provincial Park and on most trails in Herring Cove Provincial Park. Why not leave a little bit of the natural in nature?

Fortunately, the future is certain to bring more trails. Ed Melanson and Alonso Legere are actively pursuing an eastward extension of the Dobson Trail towards Sackville as well as an extension of the Fundy Footpath towards St. Martins and Saint John. At the same time, work has already begun on the extension of the famed Appalachian Trail from Mount Katahdin in Baxter State Park, Maine, through New Brunswick's Mount Carleton Provincial Park to the Chic Choc Mountains in Quebec. Without a doubt, these are exciting developments for hiking enthusiasts.

BEFORE YOU START OUT

The tourist season in New Brunswick is concentrated in July and August. Many attactions and provincial campsites open only in mid-to-late June and close around Labour Day. The hiking season is, however, considerably longer. Personally, we prefer spring and fall for hiking, to avoid crowds as well as heat, humidity and biting insects. In particular, the cool days of April to mid-May and September to the end of October (and sometimes even into November) make for excellent hiking. Mid-May is usually the time when bugs start to appear in large numbers. This onslaught lasts for some four to six weeks but does not totally vanish until the first frost. Fortunately, the mosquitoes, black flies and horse flies do not carry diseases. Also, cases of ticks carrying lyme disease are rare in New Brunswick. As a precaution, however, you should always wear protective clothing such as long sleeves and long pants and, if bitten by a tick, you should see a doctor. Along the Fundy coast and in the northern part of the province, the fly season can start a few weeks later. In the fall, Indian summer is a particularly beautiful time to hike. This usually lasts for about two weeks in early October. But remember: this is hunting season. If you decide to hike outside provincial and national parks, wear bright clothing (preferably hunter orange) to alert hunters who may mistake you for deer, moose or other game.

As with any other activity, safety is crucial. Although hiking poses relatively few hazards, it pays to know about them and take appropriate precautions. Usually, "trail safety" brings to mind hazards such as falling from a cliff or being mauled by a bear. However, another problem exists, even though it has not crossed the line from nuisance to hazard. While easy access to trails is generally a good thing, it also provides everybody with an opportunity to reach just about any point in the woods with relative ease. So far, this has fortunately re-sulted "only" in illegal and unsightly dumpsites in the woods. Similarly, theft on the trail is not a problem at present, but it does not hurt to be careful.

You needn't worry too much about four-legged ani-mals. Wild animals generally avoid humans. However, when a hiker enters an animal's fear circle, its response may be fear — the animal runs away — or anger — the animal attacks. Don't try to find out which an animal will choose! As a general rule, signal your presence by talking or by making any other noise. If you see an ani-mal, give it a wide berth. These rules are particularly important in the spring when mother bears nurse and guard their January-born young, and in the rutting sea-son of deer and moose in the fall.

Campers should avoid carrying smelly food or other items. If this cannot be avoided, seal such items in freezer bags and possibly hang them and your food pack high in a tree so that camp marauders cannot get to them. Squirrels, raccoons and other animals will chew holes in packs to get at the delicacies inside.

Pets, and especially dogs, have no place in the wilderness. Dogs, when not on a leash, may (and often do) remember their half-buried hunting instincts and go after deer and squirrels. Moreover, bears strongly dislike dogs and sometimes attack them or their companions — you. So please leave Rover at home.

One of the most feared dangers is getting lost in the woods. The worst enemy in such a situation is panic. There are reports of hunters who got lost, panicked, and shot themselves in their confusion. In New Brunswick, you can always reach some outpost of civilization within a couple of days and usually much sooner — provided, of course, that you are able to use map and compass. It is not smart to undertake a multi-day trip without some basic training in their use and such training could even come in handy on long day hikes. All better compasses (and other kinds are worthless at best and at worst outright dangerous) come with reasonably detailed instructions. Most books on hiking cover this subject; see the bibliography.

All maps in *A Hiking Guide to New Brunswick* include an arrow pointing to true north. There is roughly a 22-degree difference (declination) between true north and magnetic north, to which every compass needle points. Failure to observe this declination results in considerable error; for every three miles hiked, you will deviate from the true course by more than one mile! In addition, hikers are advised to carry a topographical (or "topo") map of areas where trails are less groomed. Some local libraries and stores carry topos; if you cannot find them locally, contact the Department of Energy, Mines, & Resources, Ottawa, Canada K1A 0E9.

Other hazards exist, among them unstable cliffs along Fundy coastlines and at some summits in Mount Carleton Provincial Park. We recommend that you stay away from the edges of cliffs. Also hazardous are the

Fundy Footpath. H.A. EISELT

high tides along the Fundy Coast. There are places where hikers may get trapped between an unscalable cliff and the rising water. None of these places is included in this book. However, for some hikes along the coast, you should carry tide tables, available from the Geographic Information Corporation at (506) 856-2322.

Another problem should be mentioned here, even though it is not so much a hazard as a nuisance. In the spring, there may be a significant amount of deadfall even on maintained trails. Typically, this is the result of storms in the previous fall, and it usually takes a while for the cleanup crews to finish their work. For safety's sake, follow the old-time lumberman's rule: don't step on anything you can step over, and don't step on anything you can step around.

Campfires must be put out before you leave your campsite. That doesn't mean they should die down to just a few embers or a little smouldering. It means OUT

COLD. The danger of forest fires in many parts of New Brunswick is amplified by the extensive planting of soft-wood forests rather than the ecologically preferable mixed woods. Actually, on day hikes fires are not needed at all, and on longer backpacking trips, light-weight white gas/naphtha or butane stoves are vastly superior to campfires as they cook much quicker and cleaner. We strongly recommend them.

Many books have been written about hiking equip-ment and this is not the place to repeat their valued advice. Some well-known references are Colin Fletcher's classic *The Complete Hiker III* as well as the books by John Hart, Harvey Manning and Bill Riviere; see the bibliography. Here, we only list a few items that we consider a must on any but the shortest hike. They include:

– FLY DOPE. Muskol and Off! have an excellent reputation. Be careful, though; their active ingredi-ent, DEET, is said to soften the brain, and it surely dissolves plastics. Keep it away from your eyes!
– FIRST AID KIT. Knowing some basics about first aid is always handy, but a first aid kit is utterly use-less if you don't know what that funny looking stuff is for.
– MAP. A topographical map, usually 1:50,000. Sometimes specialized hikers' maps are available, and they may be preferable as long as they show contour lines – a seemingly short distance can be very strenuous if it leads up and down steep hills!
– COMPASS. Get a trustworthy one and learn how to use it. Good brand names are Brunton, Silva, and Suunto.
– CANTEEN WITH WATER. The 1-litre (1-quart) size is best for day trips and the 2-litre (half gallon) size is good for backpacking trips. Bigger bottles or

canteens are usually too heavy to be useful. An alternative is to use existing sources of water and purify it. In a pinch, iodine-based purification tablets are OK, but active backpackers nowadays rely mostly on water filters such as Katadyn, MSR, PUR, First Need, or similar products.

– SUNGLASSES. For hiking in higher elevations, UV blockers are required.

– SUNSCREEN. SPF 15 is recommended.

– EXTRA CLOTHING. Socks and raingear.

– EXTRA FOOD. High-calorie snacks such as trail mix or trail bars are best.

– POCKET KNIFE. A sturdy folding knife, such as the Swiss Army knives, or mini-tools, such as Leatherman or Gerber.

– WATERPROOF MATCHES. Better yet a transparent Bic lighter (so you always know how much fuel is left).

– DAYPACK or "fanny pack" (more correctly, belly bag). Light-weight, to carry the rest of the items. Some of the more elaborate bags incorporate bottle holders.

Some words regarding wilderness etiquette are necessary. We've all heard the slogans "Take only pictures, leave only footprints" and "If you pack it in, pack it out." They basically say it all. Even "small" items such as candy wrappers and cigarette butts are eyesores and will soon give your fellow hikers the feeling of hiking on a dump. Another problem is human waste, which may not only be a disgusting sight but may also pose a health risk. When you have to go, get away from any body of water — at least 30 metres (100 ft) but preferably much farther. Otherwise, you may contaminate the water and spread diseases such as giardia. With a knife or trowel, dig a "cat hole," a small hole four to eight inches deep (any deeper and the waste will not decompose quickly). When you're finished, cover the hole and its contents, including the paper, with soil. We saw one of the worst violations of this simple process at a small campsite at a river next to a nice stand of trees. Nice it was, but closer inspection revealed that it had been used as an extensive on-ground outdoor facility. Camping nearby must have felt like sleeping and eating in a sewer.

Finally, a few remarks about the information in this book. We rehiked all the trails included in the first edition plus quite a few new trails in 1995. The descriptions and maps represent an accurate account of the trails at that time. However, trails — particularly those outside parks — may change course or become obscured because they are subject to alterations due to logging, one of New Brunswick's key industries. When lumbermen move their trucks and other heavy equipment into an area, trails and other distinctive features are invariably destroyed. On the other hand, once the forest in a logged-over area recovers over the years, old logging roads may become new hiking trails. Beaver dams, forest fires and other natural causes alter the landscape over time.

Although this edition of *A Hiking Guide to New Brunswick* is as up to date as we can make it, trail features change constantly. The climate and soil conditions of the Atlantic Northeast generate vigorous growth, so trails can become quickly overgrown and impassable if not properly maintained. Part of the maintenance is actually done by the hiking public. Using a trail keeps down the growth. As in many other instances, the saying "Use it or lose it" applies. In this book, we have not included trails that have deteriorated below a certain level where the hiker will have arduous climbs over massive deadfalls or will need rubber boots to cross swampy areas.

In the future, access roads will continue to be rebuilt, trail sections will be rerouted, trails will be reclassified and new nature walks will be constructed. In the first edition of *A Hiking Guide to New Brunswick*, we described one of the trails as passing "a very nice stand of tamaracks," which over the years has turned into "a very dead stand of tamaracks." Such changes may seem trifling to some, but to the hiker trying to find a trailhead for an afternoon stroll or an all-day walk, such changes are extremely significant. As a general precaution, hikers should not only *carry* a map and a compass but *use* them frequently.

Distances in the *Hiking Guide to New Brunswick* have been obtained from various sources, including a pedometer. **Hiking times** are, of course, highly personal. Our times are based on a somewhat relaxed pace with a few short breaks. We know that many trails could be "done" in considerably less time, but after all, this book is about hiking, not running. Once, when we remarked to a fellow hiker about someone who had hiked through the Grand Canyon from the North to the South Rim in a single day (it took us four, plus two for side trips), he replied: "So what? The mountains don't care." This pretty much reflects our attitude. We suggest that individuals hike some of the shorter trails first, keeping track of their own times. They can then find an appropriate multiplier before attempting any of the longer hikes.

The description of each trail in this book starts with a heading with some shorthand information about the trail. The hiking time and the topo maps have already been discussed. Sometimes, other useful maps exist (expecially in parks); in such cases we have indicated this. We generally distinguish between two **types of trails**: linear and loop trails. In the case of a linear trail, hikers must retrace their steps (or find some other way out); loops end at the trailhead. The **lengths** of the trails are always the distances back to the trailhead; for linear trails, they are twice the one-way distance. This way, hikers can see at a glance if a trail is suitable for them. Measuring the **ascent** of a trail is difficult: ideally, hikers would like to know the total ascent they have to climb. Here, however, we can only provide the vertical distance between the lowest and the highest elevation of a trail. The **difficulty** of a trail is measured on a scale from easy (e), to moderate (m), to strenuous (s) with intermediate degrees easy-to-moderate (e-m), and moderate-to-strenuous (m-s). Like hiking time, the difficulty of a trail is personal, so we recommend that you check your own ability and rating against ours. Information concerning the **trail condition** points out some of the obstacles found along the trail, such as wet spots or rough sections. Again, trail conditions change with the seasons; water levels tend to be higher in spring, and deadfall is likely to be gone from park trails by mid-season.

We sincerely hope that our readers will have as much fun hiking New Brunswick's trails as we had when writing this book. There's a lot to discover, and we wish you "Happy Trails" as, *A Hiking Guide to New Brunswick* in hand, you explore this beautiful province.

M. & H.A. Eiselt

ST. JOHN RIVER VALLEY

ST. JOHN RIVER VALLEY

The major feature of this region is, of course, the St. John River. Originating in northern Maine and about 724 km (450 mi) long, the river drains large areas in Western New Brunswick. Although its course has changed a few times over the millenia, the river has served as the first highway to many peoples: Maliseet Indians, Acadians, British Loyalists, Scottish, Irish and Danish settlers, and other early residents.

The river valley is very fertile and much of it is prime agricultural land. Its use changes from north to south: from the northern maple groves of the sugar-shack farmers to apple orchards and extensive potato farms and large fields with Holsteins or grain crops in the southern valley.

The region's most dramatic history took place in the northern section. After constant haggling about boundaries between Canada and the United States in the 1800s, the people of the area opted to declare themselves independent and proclaimed the Republic of Madawaska with the town of Edmundston as its capital. Though never truly independent, the area has retained its own distinct character. Traces of the past are still encountered in the crafts of the valley's artisans. Remnants of old sawmills evoke the memory of John Glasier and other lumbermen who exploited one of New Brunswick's richest resources.

Farther south, in the vicinity of Grand Falls, the riverbed widens, the woods retreat and rolling hills dominate. This is New Brunswick's potato country; small towns dot the banks of the river and farmers' markets are a frequent sight on Saturdays. At Mactaquac, a large dam was built in the 1960s to satisfy the need for electrical power. Construction of the dam was certainly an engineering feat, and it created a large lake that is used for recreational purposes. At the same time, however, it destroyed many old buildings and flooded entire villages, which required the resettling of many people. As a gesture of reconciliation, the 120 hectare (300-acre) historical settlement of Kings Landing was created, and some early settlers' houses that otherwise would have been lost were transported there.

Farther downstream, the river reaches Fredericton, the province's capital. Although some Indians, French and British had settled here, the town's history began on a large scale in 1783 when some two thousand United Empire Loyalists settled at Ste. Anne's Point. In 1785, Lt. Governor Thomas Carleton renamed it "Frederick's Town" after Frederick, second son of King George III. Later that year, Frederick's Town became the capital of the province of New Brunswick, which had been founded just one year before.

The river continues southwards, past green meadows and numerous islands, and is joined by many rivers before emptying into the Bay of Fundy.

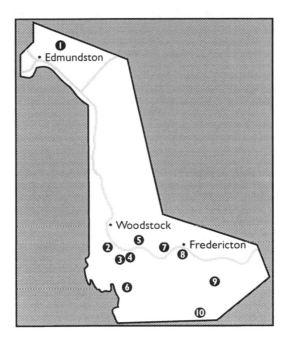

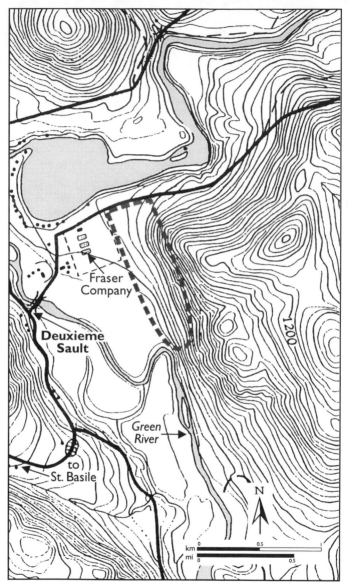

Fraser
Company

**Deuxieme
Sault**

*Green
River*

to
St. Basile

N

km
mi

Second Falls Nature Trail

Second Falls Nature Trail
(Fraser Co.)

Length: 4.2 km (2.6 mi) **Hiking Time:** 1 hr
Type: loop **Map:** 21 N/8 Edmundston
Difficulty: easy **Trail Condition:** dry
Ascent: negligible

Access: From Fredericton, take the Trans-Canada High-way (Highway 2) towards Edmundston. Before entering Edmundston, take exit 21 at St. Basile. Turn right onto Iroquois Road and follow the road for 8.4 km (5.2 mi). Keep straight at a Stop sign at Titus Road. Turn right at the next Stop sign and follow the road for 9.6 km (5.9 mi) to 2e Sault. Keep right at a fork, cross a bridge, and keep right again. The main building of the Fraser Company is located on the right across from a lake and a picnic site. Vehicles can be parked here. The trailhead is located about 200 m/yd up the road on the right side.

Trail Markings: The nature trail is unmarked but obvious. An explanatory booklet is sometimes available in a box at the trailhead.

The Trail: The trail winds through young white spruce and passes a small open area before turning left into mixed woods. The path ascends and reaches a small picnic site. Just beyond, a shortcut departs to the right. The main trail continues straight, crosses a suspension bridge, and descends on boardwalks and wooden steps to a stream with a picnic site. Continue on the board-walk and turn right immediately at its end. The trail first leads along the edge of a nursery before being joined by a dirt road from the left. From here, the trail returns past large greenhouses to the main road.

Trail Features: The brochure describes many of the plants and animals that make these New Brunswick woods their home. Among them are yellow clintonias (whose crushed leaves provide a potent insect repellent), hazelnut trees, conks (fungi that grows on trees), lichen and old-man's beard. Even without the brochure, a multitude of signs point out different species of trees along the nature walk. Finally, glimpses into the greenhouses will reveal thousands of young spruce.

MALISEET TRAIL

Length: 3.4 km (2.1 mi) rtn [+ 1 km (0.6 mi) rtn]
Type: linear
Difficulty: easy
Ascent: 50 m (150 ft)

Hiking Time: 1 hr rtn [+ 30 min rtn]
Map: 21 J/4 Woodstock
Trail Condition: dry

Access: From Fredericton, take the Trans-Canada Highway (Highway 2) in a westerly direction for about 82 km (51 mi) to Meductic. About 5.4 km (3.4 mi) beyond exit 212 at Meductic, a marker located on the left side of the road indicates a national historic site. The trailhead, marked by a large sign saying "Maliseet Trail," is located about 400 m/yd beyond this marker. Parking is possible on the left side of the highway at the trailhead.

Trail Markings: The trail is marked by blue metal blazes with a white diagonal bar.

The Trail: This well-maintained trail gently ascends through open softwoods onto a beautiful hardwood ridge. At about 1.5 km (0.9 mi), you come to a fork. The

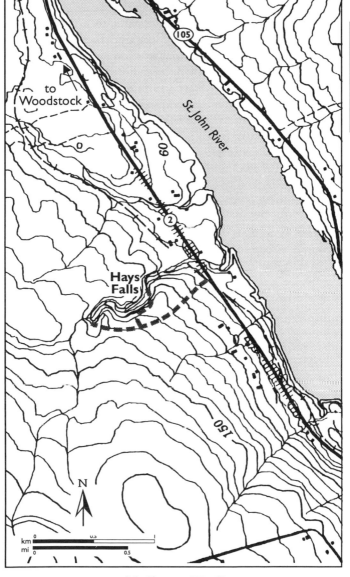

to Woodstock

St. John River

Hays Falls

N

Maliseet Trail

ST. JOHN RIVER VALLEY   45

right fork leads down to the bottom of the 27 m (90 ft) cascading Hays Falls. The left fork continues a short distance to a rocky cliff at the head of the falls. This is the end of the marked trail.

A short extension takes you to a fine view of the St. John River. Cross a little creek next to the head of the falls and continue straight on an old wagon road for some 100 m/yd to a T-junction. Turn right onto an old woods road and follow it for about 400 m/yd, where it turns left onto a tree farm. Keep to the right on a wide farm road. From here, you'll enjoy the beautiful panoramic view of the St. John River and surrounding area.

Trail Features: The waterfalls are the major attraction of this trail. The Maliseet Indian Trail, an old portage, was located in this area. It is now overgrown and logged over.

LOOKOUT NATURE TRAIL
(Big Pokiok Nature Park, St. Anne-Nackawic Pulp Co., Ltd.)

Length: 0.6 km (0.4 mi)	**Hiking Time:** 10 min
Type: loop	**Map:** 21 G/14 Canterbury,
Difficulty: easy	leaflet available at trailhead
Ascent: negligible	**Trail Condition:** crushed rock

Access: From Fredericton, take the Trans-Canada Highway (Highway 2) in a westerly direction towards Edmundston. Follow the highway for about 60 km (37 mi). Take exit 232 towards Nackawic, turn left underneath the overpass, and turn off to the right onto a dirt road as the ramp swings to the left. This is the entrance to Big Pokiok Nature Park. At 3.3 km (2.1 mi), the road crosses Big Pokiok Stream. Just beyond the wooden bridge there is a parking area to the left with two pit toilets and space for 15-20 vehicles. The trailhead is located on the left side of the parking lot.

Trail Markings: The trail is unmarked but it is impossible to miss.

Trail Features: The main features of this nature walk are the many nature displays and the access to the Big Pokiok Stream, which is particularly impressive in the spring.

STREAMSIDE NATURE TRAIL
(Big Pokiok Nature Park, St. Anne-Nackawic Pulp Co., Ltd.)

Length: 1.8 km (1.1 mi)	**Hiking Time:** 20 min
Type: loop	**Map:** 21 G/14 Canterbury,
Difficulty: easy	leaflet available at trailhead
Ascent: 20 m (60 ft)	**Trail Condition:** slippery when wet

Access: From Fredericton, take the Trans-Canada Highway (Highway 2) in a westerly direction towards Edmundston. Follow the highway for about 60 km (37 mi). Take exit 232 towards Nackawic, turn left underneath the overpass, and turn off to the right onto a dirt road as the ramp swings to the left. This is the entrance to Big Pokiok Nature Park. At 3.3 km (2.1 mi), the road crosses Big Pokiok Stream. Just beyond the wooden bridge there is a parking area to the left with two pit toilets and space for 15-20 vehicles. The trailhead is located just beyond the parking space on the right side of the road.

Trail Markings: In general, the trail is easy to follow. At some points, red blazes with arrows point the way.

The Trail: The narrow path swings into the woods, keeps right at an indistinct fork, and descends to the Big Pokiok Stream. The trail follows the stream, keeping it to the left. There are some corduroy bridges and sections across wet spots. Just before the trail reaches Pokiok Narrows Bridge, it turns right. The trail joins the road near the trailhead.

Trail Features: The main features of the trail are the Big Pokiok Stream and its streamside vegetation, including trilliums and fiddleheads in the spring. Signs along the trail point to interesting natural features ranging from a big anthill to nesting and roosting places of the pileated woodpecker.

NACKAWIC NATURE TRAIL

Length: 3.2 km (2 mi)   **Hiking Time:** 45 min
Type: loop   **Map:** 21 G/14 Canterbury
Difficulty: easy   **Trail Condition:** dry
Ascent: negligible

Access: From Fredericton, take the Trans-Canada Highway (Highway 2) in a westerly direction towards Edmundston. Follow the highway for about 60 km (37 mi). Take exit 232 towards Nackawic and cross the bridge over the St. John River. Follow the road for 3.4 km (2.1 mi), then turn right onto Landegger Drive just before an Irving gas station and follow the signs to the Nackawic Shopping Mall. Turn right at a T-junction onto Otis Drive and follow it for 0.6 km (0.4 mi). Note the big "Nackawic axe" on the left next to the river – a reminder that in 1991 the town of Nackawic was chosen "Forestry Capital of Canada." A sign to "picnic sites" on the left side of the road leads to a small parking lot for up to 10 vehicles. A display explains the route of this trail, which was opened in 1989.

Trail Markings: None, but the trail is well groomed and easy to follow.

The Trail: The wide trail slopes down towards the St. John River. Continue straight (a side trail departs to the right) and straight again at a 4-way junction. The trail passes a dilapidated structure on its left. A little below, the remains of an old homestead can still be seen to the right of the trail. The trail ends at a turnaround next to Otis Drive.

Return on the same trail to the 4-way junction. There, turn left and keep right at a fork. Turn left at a T-junction and keep right just before the trail reaches the road. From here, the trail returns to the parking lot.

Trail Features: The main attractions of this trail are the many fine views across the scenic St. John River. Picnic sites are plentiful, and in July black-eyed Susans blossom along the trail.

BOULDERWALK TRAIL

Length: 4.8 km (3 mi)
Type: loop
Difficulty: easy
Ascent: negligible

Hiking Time: 1 hr 15 min
Map: 21 G/11 McAdam
Trail Condition: dry, rocky and rooty

Access: From Fredericton, take the Trans-Canada Highway (Highway 2) in a westerly direction towards Edmundston. At Longs Creek, turn onto Highway 3 south and follow it to Thomaston Corner, where you turn off onto Highway 4. Drive through the town of McAdam and continue on Highway 4 for 6.9 km (4.3 mi), measured from the historic railway station. Turn right onto Highway 630 north towards Canterbury and follow this graded dirt road for 3.1 km (1.9 mi). Then turn left onto another dirt road, which leads into Spednic Lake Provincial Park. Follow this road to a T-junction at the lake. Several vehicles can park in the area. To reach the trailhead, turn right onto the road that leads to the campsites. The clearly marked trailhead is located on the right.

Trail Markings: The trail is marked by 2" x 2" blue metal blazes with a white diagonal bar, as well as 2" x 2" yellow metal blazes.

The Trail: The narrow but well-defined path traverses a nice hardwood ridge and passes through mixed forest before reaching an observation deck with interpretive plaques at 1.3 km (0.8 mi). This place offers good views across the swamps and the Little Digdeguash River. Retrace your steps and turn right to follow the loop trail. The level path passes another interpretive plaque and makes a sharp left turn at the tip of the peninsula. Enjoy the view across Diggity Cove and Spednic Lake, which has several islands and a number of larger boulders deposited by glaciation. The trail continues to another fine lookout, then passes one of those big boulders in the woods before reaching a wide dirt road at the campground. Turn left, pass two pit toilets, and return to the trailhead.

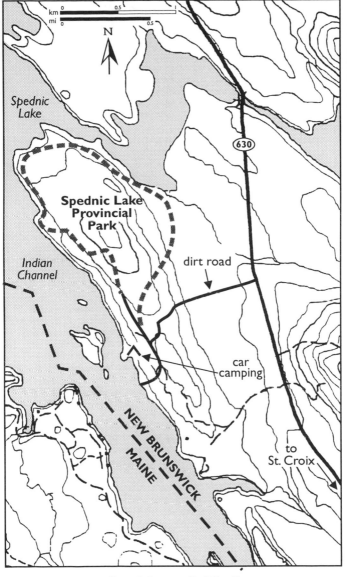

Boulderwalk Trail

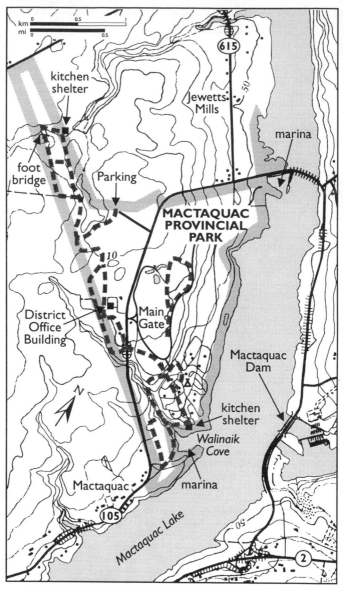

Mactaquac Provincial Park

Trail Features: This trail leads through parts of the St. Croix Heritage River System which was shaped by the last ice age. This area was populated by various native peoples as early as 11,000 years ago. The lookout at a swamp along the trail is a peaceful place where wildlife can be observed. Spednic Lake's remarkable glacial boulders and the cool breeze off its waters add to the attraction of the trail.

MACTAQUAC PROVINCIAL PARK

Mactaquac Provincial Park was established in the 1960s. The park comprises 560 hectares (1,400 acres) and its dominant feature is the Mactaquac headpond. The headpond features two supervised beaches as well as marinas for sail and power boats, and fishing, swimming and waterskiing are permitted. In addition, the park offers a campground with 300 sites, a picnic area and an 18-hole golf course.

You reach the park from Fredericton by taking the Trans-Canada Highway (Highway 2) west towards Edmundston. About 18 km (11 mi) from Fredericton, take exit 274 and follow Highway 105, which first crosses Mactaquac Dam and later a causeway. The main entrance to the park is 7.4 km (4.5 mi) from the Trans-Canada Highway, on the left side of the road.

BEAVER POND TRAIL

(including Beaver Pond Nature Trail, Little Mactaquac
Nature Trail, and Porcupine Path Trail)

Length: 5 km (3 mi)   **Hiking Time:** 1 hr 30 min
Type: loop   **Map:** 21 G/15 Fredericton
Difficulty: easy   **Trail Condition:** dry
Ascent: negligible

Access: On Highway 105, park at a gate on the right
side of the road a short distance behind a water tower
at a hiking sign, about 0.9 km (0.5 mi) before the main
park entrance. If the gate is open, drive to the end of
the 700 m/yd gravel road to a parking lot and picnic
site, and start the trail from there.

Trail Markings: The trails are marked by metal blazes
with black or white diagonal stripes. The blazes for Beaver
Pond Nature Trail are orange, those for Little Mactaquac Nature Trail and Porcupine Path Trail are yellow,
and the connecting trails are blazed in red.

The Trail: Pass through the gate and follow the gravel
road for 700 m/yd. Just before you reach a parking lot and
a picnic area, turn left onto a gravel trail. (If the gate is
open, you may begin your hike at the parking lot by walking back towards the gate and then turning right onto the
Beaver Pond Nature Trail.) A beaver pond soon becomes
visible on the right where a bridge across the pond provides a shortcut. Follow the trail around the pond and,
at 0.6 km (0.4 mi), turn right at a fork. (The left fork connects with the Alex Creek Trail). Continue until you reach
a woods road. Here the Beaver Pond Nature Trail ends.

Turn left onto Old Moore Road and continue; you
are now on the Little Mactaquac Nature Trail. Just before the wide road leaves the forest and becomes more

open, the trail turns off the road to the right and a short-cut soon departs to the right. Follow the main trail and cross the weathered bridge that spans the Little Mactaquac River. The trail then follows the creek for the next little while. At one point it ascends steeply and then immediately descends to the level of the water. Soon after that you reach a fork. A short spur to the left leads to a kitchen shelter with a barbecue pit where there are often signs of porcupine activity around the hut. The main trail continues on the right.

Take the bridge across the creek and follow the yellow blazes. Boardwalks form many sections of the trail in this area. At a sign, turn left onto a small side trail. This is the Porcupine Path Trail, a short and less-well-maintained side trail which ends at the beaver pond, where the extensive work of beavers can be observed. Return to the main trail and turn left. The trail soon ends farther down along the beaver pond. Turn left and return to the parking lot at the gate.

Trail Features: The trail provides good opportunities to watch the work of the beaver. There are also many signs of porcupine, deer and moose. Red-winged blackbirds, ducks and woodpeckers are frequently seen at the pond.

ALEX CREEK TRAIL

Length: 2.2 km (1.4 mi)   **Hiking Time:** 45 min
Type: loop   **Map:** 21 G/15 Fredericton
Difficulty: easy   **Trail Condition:** dry
Ascent: 10 m (30 ft)

Access: On Highway 105, turn right and proceed to a building with a sign that reads "District Office," about

100 m/yd before the main gate. Parking is at the back of the building.

Trail Markings: The trail is marked by 3" x 3" blue metal blazes, occasionally with white or black diagonal stripes. Connectors are marked by red metal blazes.

The Trail: Cross the field at the far end of the parking lot to the sign for Alex Creek Trail, which is visible from the parking lot. The trail passes through old cedars and then leads into the woods. At a T-junction, the trail turns to the left and continues along easy grades. At first the forest consists mostly of spruce and fir; later it changes to birch and aspen. At some point you will see a hut to the right in a small valley below the trail. Soon the path crosses Alex Creek for the first time. Beyond the bridge, take the right fork. (The left fork connects to the Jones Field Trail. This 0.7 km (0.4 mi) connecting trail is marked by red blazes with white diagonals.) The trail follows the creek and crosses it again. The trail soon leads to the hut you saw earlier, which is equipped with benches and a barbecue pit.

The trail continues past a pile of rocks and later crosses a stone wall. These are the remains of farms and fields that settlers worked in bygone days. Just beyond the stone wall, the trail continues straight at a junction. (The right fork is a shortcut to the parking lot.) After 500 m/yd, the trail reaches another junction. The left fork connects to the Beaver Pond Nature Trail; this connector is marked by red blazes. Continue straight ahead through a pretty stand of aspen. At the next fork, bear to the left. The trail eventually leads back to the parking lot.

Trail Features: The woods trail follows a creek, and woodpeckers and porcupines can occasionally be seen.

MAPLE SUGAR TRAIL

Length: 1.8 km (1.1 mi)   **Hiking Time:** 20 min
Type: loop   **Map:** 21 G/15 Fredericton
Difficulty: easy   **Trail Condition:** dry
Ascent: negligible

Access: Enter the park through the main gate and immediately turn right. Follow the paved road for 0.9 km (0.5 mi) to where another road joins from the right. The trailhead is located on the left of the main road. To reach the parking lot, turn right towards the campground.

Trail Markings: The trail is unmarked but obvious and cannot be missed.

The Trail: The path ascends gently through a mature mixed forest and crosses two wide woods roads in its course. The trail ends where it leaves the woods and arrives at an open field. At this point you have a good view to the right of the Mactaquac headpond and the dam. Turn right onto a small road that follows the edge of the woods. After some 250 m/yd, the path ends at a gate and the trail turns right onto a blacktop road. Follow this road for 0.5 km (0.3 mi) back to the trailhead near the parking lot.

Trail Features: The main feature of this nature trail is the large variety of trees that make up the surrounding mature forest. Sugar maples abound. These trees have been a source of sugar for North American Indians for hundreds of years; their sap is used to produce the always popular maple syrup.

JONES FIELD – MARINA TRAIL

Length: 3.2 km (2 mi)   **Hiking Time:** 45 min
Type: loop   **Map:** 21 G/15 Fredericton
Difficulty: easy to   **Trail Condition:** dry
moderate
Ascent: 20 m (60 ft)

Access: Enter the park through the main gate and immediately turn right. Follow the paved road for 0.9 km
(0.5 mi). Turn right again and pass through the gate to
the campground. Turn right again and continue on the
campground road to a gate next to campsite #90. This
is the location of the trailhead.

Trail Markings: The trail is marked by white triangles
with black diagonals.

The Trail: The trail first passes through a gate and follows a descending woods road. Just beyond a kitchen
shelter (with tables, sinks and a fine view across Walinaik Cove) the trail reaches the cove, which it follows
for a while. The trail turns left, crosses a bridge over
Alex Creek, which flows into the cove, and reaches a
fork. Keep left and begin the Marina Loop Trail (you will
return to this fork later). The trail ascends some wooden
steps, turns left at a landing, and crosses a small wooden
bridge at the head of a 10 m (30 ft) waterfall. Keep left
when the path reaches a clearing. When the trail approaches a paved road, turn left towards the marina
and enter the woods to the left just as the road reaches
the cove. The path skirts the cove, passes the foot of the
waterfall and finally reaches the bridge and the fork.

Continue straight at the fork. Here the trail follows
Alex Creek, crossing the shady creek three times on
wooden bridges until it finally reaches a 4-way junc-

tion. Straight ahead is the campground and on the left is the connector to the Alex Creek Trail, but the Jones Field Trail continues to the right. The trail reaches the paved road at campsite #62. Turn right and follow the road for some 150 m/yd to the trailhead.

Trail Features: The major features of this trail are a number of fine views across Walinaik Cove and the Mactaquac headpond and a close-up look at a waterfall.

ODELL PARK LOOP

Length: 5.2 km (3.2 mi)   **Hiking Time:** 1 hr 45 min
Type: loop   **Map:** 21 G/15 Fredericton
Difficulty: easy to   **Trail Condition:** some wet
moderate   spots
Ascent: 30 m (100 ft)

Access: From downtown Fredericton, drive uphill on Smythe Street and turn right at the traffic lights onto Waggoners Lane. After 0.5 km (0.3 mi), turn left into the Odell Park parking lot.

Trail Markings: The trail is unmarked, but towards its end it follows the Arboretum Nature Trail, which is marked by signs displaying a hiker.

The Trail: Walk up to the lodge and start the trail at the sign saying "Nature Path" at the second trail to the right, as seen from the lodge. Follow the wide woods trail, ignore the first departing trail to the left, and after 300 m/yd, turn left at a junction. The trail leads towards Hanwell Road but, just before reaching it, swings back into the park. Keep right at two consecutive junctions

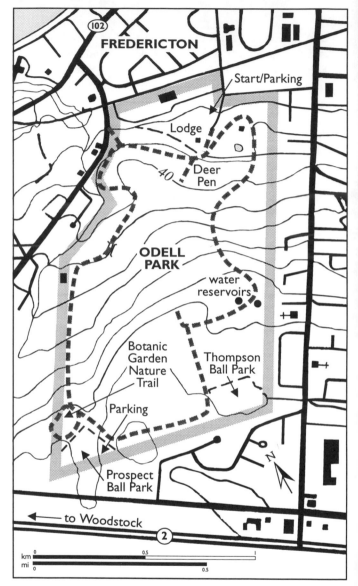

Odell Park Loop

and continue straight after a bridge. At 1.3 km (0.8 mi), the trail arrives at an open area with the Fredericton Botanic Garden Resource Centre; turn left and ascend gradually along the edge of the woods. Turn back for a good view across the St. John River Valley. Turn right at a junction onto the "Woodland Fern Trail" at a wooden sign. The short nature trail first descends and then climbs and ends at a ballpark on Prospect Street.

Turn left and connect with the gravelly trail that leads to the entrance of the Fredericton Botanic Garden and parking lot, then turn back into the woods at the edge of the parking lot at 2.4 km (1.5 mi). Continue on the main trail until at 3 km (1.9 mi), about 150 m/yds before reaching the Thompson ballpark, you turn left and follow the wide trail to a junction at 3.5 km (2.2 mi). Turn right and at 4 km (2.5 mi), you reach two water towers. Turn left here. The trail leads through a beautiful stand of beeches. After 400 m/yds, turn right onto a narrower trail. The descending trail immediately crosses the Arboretum Nature Trail, marked by a sign with a hiker. Turn right onto the nature trail and follow it to its end at the parking lot.

Trail Features: Along this old-forest loop, interpretive signs at the Botanical Garden and the Arboretum Nature Trail indicate different species of trees, shrubs and ferns native to New Brunswick. Some trees are 400 years old. The park also features a duck pond, pony stables, a deer pen, a lodge and a picnic area.

MOUNT DOUGLAS BALD TRAIL

Length: 2.5 km (1.6 mi) rtn
Type: linear
Difficulty: moderate
Ascent: 200 m (650 ft)

Hiking Time: 1 hr rtn
Map: 21 G/8 Saint John
Trail Condition: dry, rocky

Access: From Fredericton, take Highway 101 south towards Saint John, to Welsford. In Welsford, just before the junction of Highway 101 and Highway 7, turn left to the school. Parking is available in front of the building. The trail begins directly behind the school.

Trail Markings: There are no signs, but the trail is easy to find without them.

The Trail: From the right side of the schoolyard behind the building, turn left onto a dirt road, and after some 100 m/yd pass a number of unsightly old vehicles. Turn right and the trail ascends immediately. In the spring, bunchberries and lady's slippers are in bloom. The trail climbs continuously and the last section is quite steep. From the top, you is rewarded with a great view of the town of Welsford, the wooded hills around it, and Grand Bay in the distance.

Trail Features: Many woodland wildflowers are found along this rocky trail. Its major feature, however, is the magnificent view from the top that makes the short and relatively steep trail worthwhile.

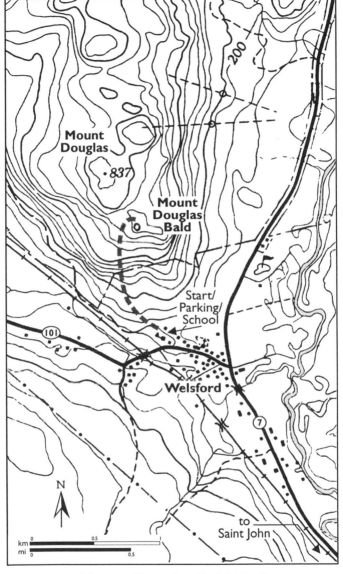

Mount Douglas Bald Trail

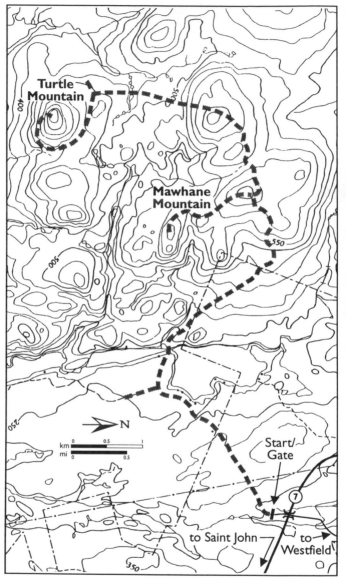

Turtle Mountain Trail

TURTLE MOUNTAIN TRAIL

Length: 20.8 km (13 mi) rtn [+ side trail 3.2 km (2 mi) rtn]
Type: linear
Difficulty: moderate
Ascent: 220 m (600 ft)

Hiking Time: 9 hrs rtn [+ 1 hr rtn]
Map: 21 G/8 Saint John
Trail Condition: a few mudholes, rocky

Access: From Fredericton, take Highway 7 south to Welsford. From the Irving station at Welsford, continue on Highway 7 in a southerly direction. After 7 km (4.4 mi), turn left onto Highway 177 towards Westfield. Follow this road for 4.4 km (2.75 mi) to a blind hill. On the left side of the road is F. Harris's house with its yellow mailbox, and on the right is a dirt road that turns back somewhat. Take this road, pass a small parking area, keep right when the road forks and pass by a private house on the right. The dirt road continues through woods, passes through a gate (we were assured that it is never closed), crosses an old log dam, and reaches an underpass under Highway 7. Just beyond the underpass, park anywhere on the left. The trailhead is located on the far left at a gate that is frequently closed. The distance from Highway 177 to this gate is about 1.9 km (1.2 mi).

Trail Markings: None, except for some occasional blue paint blazes on trees. The trail is maintained by four-wheelers and is generally easy to find. There are, however, a number of spurs that may be confusing. When in doubt, take the wider and more frequently used trail.

The Trail: Passing through the gate, the trail follows a wide dirt road. The road ascends, goes underneath some power lines, and passes a few cottages on both sides. Follow the main trail until, at 3 km (1.9 mi), you reach a narrow bridge. Vehicles other than four-wheelers cannot get beyond this point. The bridge crosses a narrow connection between Robin Hood Lake on the right and Little John Lake on the left.

The rocky trail first ascends in a northwesterly direction. At a fork, keep to the right, as this path is drier. Upon reaching a former clearing, you can see two unnamed hills to the left. The trail crosses an old logging road, continues straight ahead, and then swings to the left as an overgrown spur turns off to the right.

After a while, the trail leaves the woods and continues in a westerly direction. It is more open now, the highland landscape being covered with carpets of sheep laurels, Irish moss and black spruce. At 6.1 km (3.8 mi), you reach a plateau. Here the main trail continues straight, and a smaller side trail turns off to the left.

The spur to the left (in a southerly direction) briefly descends before it climbs to its end on Mawhane Mountain. Locals have given the hill the more colourful name "Execution Mountain," as legend has it that this is the place where sheep once accidentally fell down the steep cliffs. The side trail from the plateau to Mawhane Mountain is a 3.2 km (2 mi) detour.

Back at the plateau, continue straight ahead beyond another trail to the left which connects with the spur; the trails form a triangle. At a fork beyond the triangle, you may keep either right or left as both trails soon come together again. The trail dips down to some big mud puddles and then ascends again. Keep left at a fork and continue on the wider trail, which is quite rooty in this area. The trail continues up and down through a

Mount Douglas Bald. H.A. EISELT

nice open stand of birch trees, and then ascends again, passing through a few mudholes.

Pass a number of spurs that turn off to the right; when in doubt, keep left. The trail, which now has turned in a southerly direction, descends gently but continuously through fairly dense forest before it reaches a brook. Beyond the crossing, the trail first ascends through another stand of beautiful birch trees and a few ups and downs, then ascends more steeply. The trail continues straight (another trail turns off to the right), leads through hay-scented fern, and finally reaches a rocky area. From here, the trail climbs rather steeply to the summit of Turtle Mountain.

At the summit, there is not only a flag but also a wooden box containing notes left by previous hikers and four-wheelers. Just below the summit is an established campsite for those who plan to spend the night on Turtle Mountain.

Trail Features: The main feature of this trail is the beautiful view from the top of Turtle Mountain. Turtle Lake, with its small, boggy peninsula, lies just below to the southwest, with Labrador Lake and the Sherwood and Hasty lakes in the distance, and the Big Indian Lake can be seen in a west-northwesterly direction. On a clear day you can see the Bay of Fundy. The only signs of human activity (other than possibly a cabin on one of the lakes) is the Irving smokestack in Saint John to the southeast and a few buildings in Westfield due east. There is another fine view from Mawhane Mountain at the end of the spur.

FUNDY COAST

Hole-in-the-Wall, Grand Manan. H.A. EISELT

FUNDY COAST

The Fundy Coast is shaped by the tides of the Bay of Fundy, reputed to be among the highest in the world. The first European visitor to find his way to this area was Samuel de Champlain, who built a settlement in 1604 on St. Croix Island. It proved an unfortunate choice; the soil was barren and many of his men died, victims of scurvy and the harsh Canadian winter.

The history of the area is dominated by the United Empire Loyalists who, following the American Revolution, fled to New Brunswick (then a part of Nova Scotia) and settled along the Fundy Coast. They founded St. Andrews in 1783, one of the oldest towns in the province. Also, the towns of Parrtown and Carleton were incorporated in 1785 as Saint John, the first city to do so in what is now Canada. Here, the Loyalist heritage is carried on to this day during "Loyalist Days" with music and theatre presentations in the streets and people dressed in period costumes. The alert visitor will also notice that the pathways across King Square follow the design of the Union Jack.

In addition to a rich history, the coast also has a lot to offer naturalists, including the Fundy Isles: Deer Island, Campobello Island and Grand Manan. Whale watching and birding are favourite pastimes. In addition, Deer Island boasts the world's largest lobster pond, and "Old Sow," the world's second-largest whirlpool, which owes its existence to the Fundy tides. Campobello Island offers a provincial and an international park with beaches, rugged coastline and trails through woods. The island of Grand Manan is known for its variety of wildflowers, including orchids. The tiny community of Dark Harbour calls itself the "dulse capital of the world." Lobster ponds, herring weirs and salmon pens provide the mainstays of the island's economy.

ROOSEVELT CAMPOBELLO INTERNATIONAL PARK & HERRING COVE PROVINCIAL PARK

Campobello Island is located in the Bay of Fundy next to the town of Lubec, Maine. The French were the first European settlers, but the British established settlements around 1758. The Nova Scotia government awarded a number of land grants in 1766, one of which was an island given to Captain W. Owen for his service in the navy. In honour of its donor, Governor W. Campbell, Captain Owen called the island Campo-Bello. The island remained in the Owen family for more than a hundred years; it was then sold to a Boston firm which developed it as a summer resort. Campobello remained part of Nova Scotia until 1784, when the province of New Brunswick was founded.

Today, the island of Campobello boasts two parks: Roosevelt Campobello International Park at the southern tip of the island, and Herring Cove Provincial Park directly north of it. The 1,040-hectare (2,600-acre) Roosevelt Campobello International Park was established in 1964 and is jointly administered by Canada and the United States. The main feature of the park is the 34-room Roosevelt summer cottage where FDR spent most summers during his first 40 years. A nearby visitor centre displays historical photographs of this era.

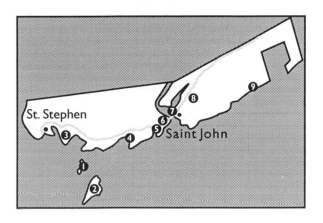

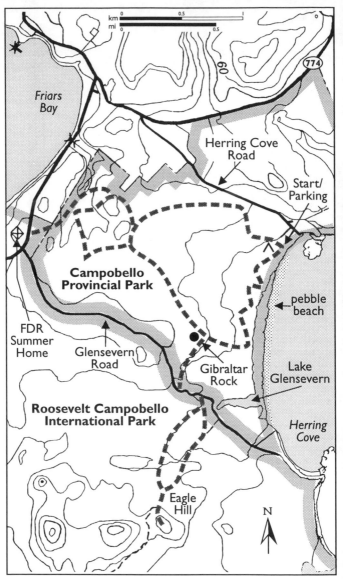

Roosevelt Cottage Loop

Next to the Roosevelt cottage is the Hubbard cottage, the summer retreat of another wealthy American family. Farther north-northeast, Herring Cove Provincial Park features a large campground, hiking trails, a long beach along the bay, and a huge boulder, a souvenir of the last ice age which formed this area.

Both parks can be reached by driving from New Brunswick through the state of Maine. To do so, cross the border at St. Stephen/Calais, then follow Highway 1 south to the town of Whiting. Turn left onto Highway 189 and drive to Lubec. Cross the border again (back into Canada) over the Roosevelt International Bridge. Remember to carry appropriate identification for the border crossings. Alternatively, you can first take a toll-free ferry from Letete, N.B., to Deer Island, N.B., and then take the toll ferry to Campobello. The latter trip is only possible during the summer months when the East Coast ferry operates; for information call (506) 747-2159.

ROOSEVELT COTTAGE LOOP
(with Gibraltar Rock and Eagle Hill side trails)
(Herring Cove Provincial Park)

Length: 7.2 km (4.5 mi) [+ 3.3 km (2 mi) side trails]
Type: loop
Difficulty: easy to moderate
Ascent: negligible

Hiking Time: 3 hrs [+ 1 hr 20 min side trails]
Map: 21 B/14 Campobello
Trail Condition: dry

Access: Beyond the customs house, follow Highway 774 for 4 km (2.5 mi). Turn right and stay on Highway 774 towards Herring Cove Provincial Park. Keep right at a fork and follow Herring Cove Road to a large parking lot at the beach on Herring Cove. There are quite a few picnic sites and facilities. The trailhead is located to the right of the parking lot.

Trail Markings: Most of the trail is marked with blue metal 3" x 3" blazes.

The Trail: The trail turns into the woods just beyond the first picnic site. Cross a dirt road and continue straight. Soon the trail reaches a T-junction at a road at the campground. Turn right and take the next road to the left. Follow this road to campsite #27 and when the road turns left, follow the narrow trail that turns off to the right. From here on the footpath is clearly marked by blue metal blazes and a sign saying "Adams' Promenade to Roosevelt Cottage." The trail leads through mixed woods, and there are some boardwalks across the muddier sections. Turn left where the path joins an old woods road. At 1.7 km (1.1 mi) you reach a 4-way junction. Continue straight ahead, cross a number of wooden bridges, and turn right at another fork.

The trail skirts a little beaver pond on its left. Shortly beyond, a side trail departs to the right (it leads to the Adams Estate, which is a lodge and restaurant). Turn onto the narrow trail to the left. After several boardwalk sections, you reach a 4-way junction. Here the trail turns right, continues through softwoods and eventualy reaches Highway 774 at 2.9 km (1.8 mi). Turn left, follow the highway to just beyond the "50" speed-limit sign, cross the highway and walk down some steps that lead directly to the Hubbard Cottage. Continue to the left towards the Roosevelt Cottage and the visitor centre.

Return to the highway, cross it, and re-enter the woods at the same spot you exited them earlier. After some 300 m/yds you arrive at a junction; keep straight and, just beyond, turn off to the right. This pretty section of the trail follows an old moss-covered carriage road that leads through softwoods.

At 4.9 km (3.1 mi) you reach a T-junction where the trail turns right to the wide Lake Glensevern Trail. Here the trail leads through hardwoods, mostly yellow birch and striped maple. Keep straight at a turnoff to the right. You reach another 4-way junction at 6.1 km (3.8 mi); here the main trail turns to the left. (A side trail continues straight ahead. It is described below.) After some 200 m/yd, a short spur to the right leads to the edge of Glensevern Lake. The main trail turns sharply to the left, continues through mixed woods and passes a small pond that is usually a home to beaver. The trail terminates at the far end of the parking lot.

Side trails: The trail straight ahead is a side trail that passes by Gibraltar Rock and finally leads to the Eagle Hill Nature Trail. The huge Gibraltar Rock becomes visible to the right of the trail a short distance beyond the 4-way junction. Adventurous hikers can climb the Rock of Gibraltar from the rear where a rope has been attached to a tree. Continue on this trail until it reaches a wide road. Turn left, and soon the Eagle Hill Nature Trail departs to the right. Follow this trail on a boardwalk through a bog. Towards its end this short nature trail makes a sharp left turn and starts ascending. It ends at a platform overlooking the bog, beach, and park. Back at the 4-way junction, turn right and continue along the main trail.

Trail Features: The main attractions of the trail are the Roosevelt Cottage, the glacial Gibraltar Rock formation, and the Eagle Hill Nature Trail and lookout. The park's visitor centre, the Roosevelt Cottage, and part of the Hubbard Cottage are open to visitors during the summer months.

UPPER DUCK POND TRAIL
(Roosevelt Campobello International Park)

Length: 5 km (3.1 mi)   **Map:** 21 B/14 Campobello
Type: loop   **Hiking Time:** 1 hr 45 min
Difficulty: easy   **Trail Condition:** wet in
Ascent: negligible   places

Access: Park at the visitor centre at the FDR Memorial Bridge. The trailhead is to the right of the road.

Trail Markings: None, but the trail is relatively easy to follow.

The Trail: From the visitor centre, the trail descends through an open field parallel to the road and in the direction of the bridge. Keep left, and about 15 m (50 ft) beyond an orange naval sign, the trail turns left into the woods. It stays close to the coast and offers occasional views over Deep Cove. At 1.1 km (0.7 mi) you reach an open field that used to be the location of the Fox Farm. The trail soon crosses a road at a field with a picnic site. Follow the "Upper Duck Pond" sign.

After crossing the open field, the trail enters softwoods, keeping a salt marsh to its left. The trail continues on an old woods road. Along the way, two small side trails depart to the left. They lead to the Lubec Channel at Upper Duck Pond. Just beyond a boardwalk section, you reach a road. Continue on that road until it reaches the Cranberry Point parking space, about 250 m/yd. Some wooden steps lead to the beach. Follow the beach for about 50 m/yd, then take the steps on the right. The trail skirts the bay, winding first through softwoods and then a stand of mountain ash. In the fall, its berries are found all along the trail. At 3.4 km (2.1 mi), the trail reaches a dirt road and fol-

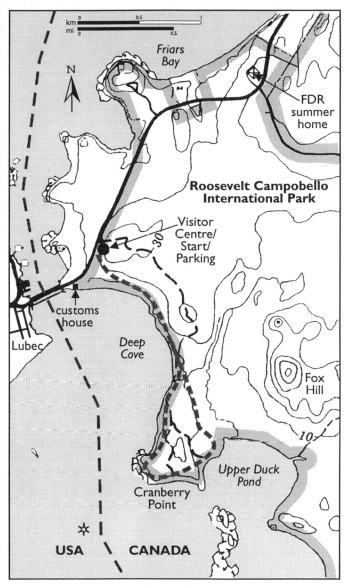

Upper Duck Pond Trail

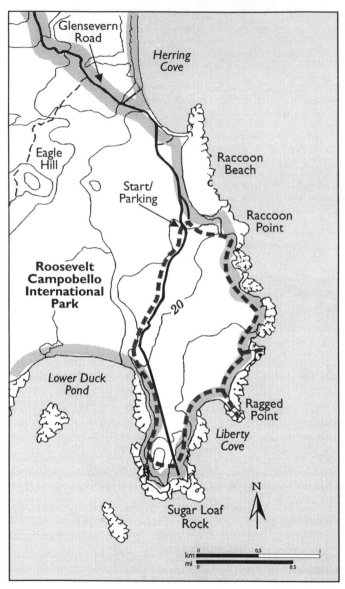

Glensevern Road

Herring Cove

Eagle Hill

Raccoon Beach

Start/ Parking

Raccoon Point

Roosevelt Campobello International Park

20

Lower Duck Pond

Ragged Point

Liberty Cove

N

Sugar Loaf Rock

km
mi

Lower Duck Pond Trail

lows it for 500 m/yd. Just beyond the picnic site at the Fox Farm, the trail turns off the road to the left and returns to the visitor centre the same way it came.

Trail Features: The trail provides frequent access to the Lubec Channel with its impressive tides and saltwater cove with waterfowl and shore birds.

Fundy Coast

LOWER DUCK POND TRAIL
(Roosevelt Campobello International Park)

Length: 6 km (3.7 mi) **Hiking Time:** 2 hrs
Type: loop **Map:** 21 B/14 Campobello
Difficulty: easy to **Trail Condition:** some wet
moderate spots, rooty
Ascent: 30 m (100 ft)

Access: From the customs house, continue straight ahead on Highway 774 for 2.3 km (1.4 mi). Turn right onto Glensevern Road and follow it for about 2.8 km (1.7 mi). Turn right onto Liberty Point Drive and follow it for 0.8 km (0.5 mi) until you reach Raccoon Beach. At this point the road divides into two roads and you will pass picnic sites and a pit toilet along the way. Parking is available here, anywhere off the road. The trailhead is located at the far left side of the picnic area, just before the divided roads join.

Trail Markings: None, but the trail is easy to follow.

The Trail: For the first few hundred metres/yards, the trail is a grassy, tree-lined wagonroad. As the trail approaches the tip of a peninsula, it narrows considerably and swings to the right. The trail continues along the cliffs and through softwoods high above the Grand Manan Channel. At one point, a small spur departs to the left and allows a scenic view. At 2 km (1.3 mi) another trail joins the main trail on the left, indicated by the sign saying "Sunsweep." This 300 m/yd trail leads through patches of wild roses, raspberry bushes and wildflowers to the head of Ragged Point. Here you will find a sculpture called "Sunsweep" that is aligned to the North Star, and there is also a fine view across the channel to Grand Manan Island.

The main trail continues along a gravel road to Liberty Point and its observation platform at 3.0 km (1.9 mi). Walk up the road to the right for about 200 m/yd. The trail turns left at the sign "Lower Duck Pond." At about 4 km (2.5 mi) it passes a picnic site on the right. In season, tasty raspberries are abundant. A long pebble beach soon becomes visible on the left, and the trail ends at a gravel road. From here you return on this gravel road to the Raccoon Beach picnic area.

Trail Features: Sheer cliffs, impressive views across the Grand Manan Channel and high tides are the major attractions of this trail.

GRAND MANAN ISLAND

The beautiful island of Grand Manan is located in the Bay of Fundy only a short distance from the coast of Maine. The first people to visit it were Passamaquoddy Indians, who came in summer to collect the eggs of gull, tern and eider. They called the island "mun a nouk," meaning "island in the sea." Narrative accounts by the French explorer Samuel de Champlain tell of a stormy night on March 16, 1606, when he was driven ashore on one of the islands south of Grand Manan. He added the word "Grand" to "menan," the French corruption of the local Indian name.

In the 17th and 18th centuries, Grand Manan was tossed back and forth between France and England, depending on who came out the winner in their frequent wars. When the American Revolution broke out, three families fled to Grand Manan for peace and shelter; however, they returned to the mainland the next year. On May 6, 1784, 50 Loyalist families arrived on the island and this date became the historic birthday of Grand Manan. After 1812, there was haggling between Great Britain and the United States over the ownership of Grand Manan. Not until 1842 was the boundary between the U.S. and Canada settled beyond doubt. Most of today's 2,500 residents are descendants of the United Empire Loyalists.

The main economy for the islanders is based on lobster and herring fishing. A modern processing plant is located at Seal Cove. Grand Manan also boasts the dulse (edible seaweed) capital of the world in Dark Harbour.

The island is composed of a unique blend of geological formations: the east side is volcanic and the west side is sedimentary rock. The two formations meet quite visibly at the Red Point Cliffs, not far from Anchorage Provincial Park. Lava flows make up other features of Grand Manan, the most spectacular being the Seven Days Work. Here, layers of lava were pushed apart by igneous intrusion, a process in which hot molten rock forces its way between layers of existing rock.

Idyllic Grand Manan is well known for bird-watching; about 250 species, including guillemots, puffins, hawks, ospreys and arctic terns have been sighted here and on the islands nearby. James Audubon drew some of his famous sketches here. Whale watching, photog-

Swallowtail Lighthouse. H.A. EISELT

raphy and, of course, hiking are popular tourist pastimes on the island.

Grand Manan is reached from mainland New Brunswick via Blacks Harbour, an important sardine-processing centre located about 130 km (80 mi) from Fredericton and 80 km (50 mi) from Saint John. From Saint John, take Highway 1 in a westerly direction and follow it to the junction with Highway 776. Turn left onto that road to Blacks Harbour which immediately makes a sharp right turn. Follow the signs to the ferry south of town. A toll ferry operates year-round from three to five times daily between Blacks Harbour on the mainland and North Head on Grand Manan; the trip takes about an hour and a half. For information regarding ferry schedules, call Coastal Transport at (506) 636-3922.

Lighthouse Trail
(in 7 sections)

Length: 36.4 km (22.6 mi)
Type: linear
Difficulty: moderate
Ascent: 160 m (530 ft)

Hiking Time: 2 days, one way
Map: 21 B/15 Campobello and 21 B/10 Grand Manan
Trail Condition: boggy spots

Summary:
Section 1: 4 km (2.5 mi), 1 hr 45 min with side trail to Hay Point
Section 2: 8 km (5 mi), 3 hrs 30 min
Section 3: 2 km (1.2 mi), 1 hr 30 min
Section 4: 6.4 km (4 mi), 2 hr 45 min
Section 5: 4.5 km (2.8 mi), 2 hrs to The Crossing, 4.3 km (2.7 mi), 2 hrs 15 min to The Whistle.
Section 6: 5.6 km (3.5 mi), 2 hrs 15 min
Section 7: 3.6 km (2.2 mi), 2 hrs
The entire trail: 36.4 km (22.6 mi)

Access: From the ferry terminal, follow Highway 776 south for about 29 km (18 mi) to its end at the Southwest Head Lighthouse. There is space for about six vehicles. The trailhead is located just north of the foghorn. The trail ends at the Swallowtail Lighthouse. There are a few parking spaces.

Trail Markings: The trail is marked by red metal discs with occasional orange blazes.

The Trail:
Section 1: SOUTHWEST HEAD LIGHTHOUSE TO BRADFORD COVE. The trail follows the edge of the cliffs in a northerly direction through heath and dwarf alder bushes. The views are spectacular. At 0.9 km (0.6 mi), the wide

trail leaves the immediate vicinity of the coast and heads through some softwoods. Muddy spots along the trail may be bypassed on narrow side trails. At 2 km (1.2 mi), just before the trail reaches Bradford Cove Pond at a camp, turn left onto a faint path. The path swings to the right, traverses a small meadow, turns right again, and crosses a ravine on a small bridge. At a junction, a very short spur departs to a lookout at Spring Rocks. The main trail continues to the right, then turns left at a T-junction onto a wide trail which it leaves shortly after to the left at a wooden sign. At the edge of a big meadow, signs point to Bradford Cove (straight) and Hay Point (slightly to the left).

The short but somewhat steep side trail to Hay Point is very worthwhile. It enters the woods and descends steeply through a grassy field to Hay Point. This picturesque lookout has a picnic table and offers a good opportunity for whale watching.

The main trail to Bradford Cove crosses the meadow and enters the woods on the other side of the field. Skirt a ravine, turn left and cross a brook. At 4 km (2.5 mi) you reach a junction just above Bradford Cove. The trail to the right, an access trail to Highway 776 at the dip at Deep Cove, is marked by red discs. The main trail continues straight towards Big Head. To explore the beach, you may climb down a wooden ladder to Bradford Cove.

Section 2: BRADFORD COVE TO DWELLYS COVE. At Bradford Cove, follow the sign towards Pandora Head and Big Cove. The red-blazed path crosses a brook, then parallels the coast and becomes less defined. At a field with an old cabin, the trail continues behind the cabin and leads straight into the woods at a red disc on a tree.

The path leads inland and turns left. It alternates between woods and small fields, allowing occasional

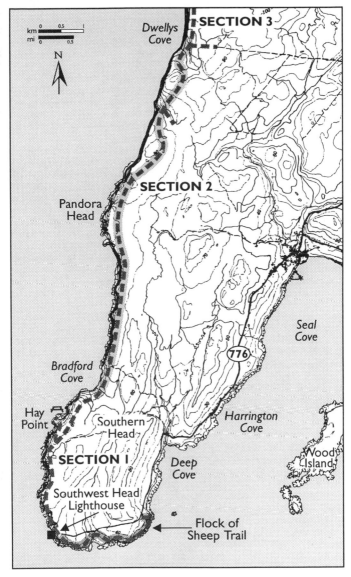

Lighthouse Trail (sections 1, 2, 3), Flock of Sheep Trail

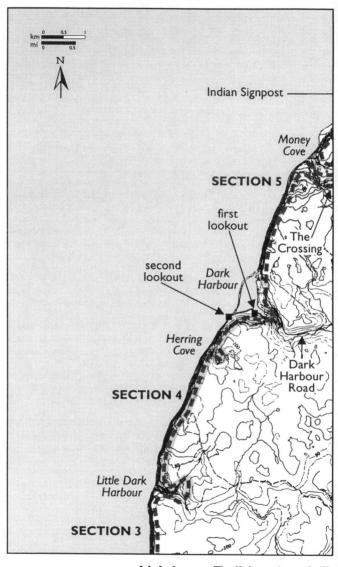

Indian Signpost

Money
Cove

SECTION 5

first
lookout

The
Crossing

second
lookout

*Dark
Harbour*

*Herring
Cove*

Dark
Harbour
Road

SECTION 4

*Little Dark
Harbour*

SECTION 3

Lighthouse Trail (sections 3-7),

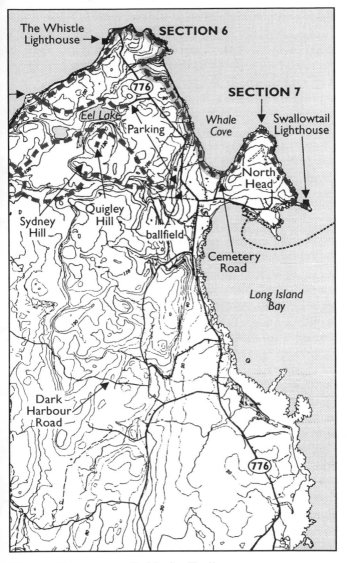

The Whistle
Lighthouse →

SECTION 6

776

Eel Lake

Parking

SECTION 7

*Whale
Cove*

Swallowtail
Lighthouse

North
Head

Sydney
Hill

Quigley
Hill

ballfield

Cemetery
Road

*Long Island
Bay*

Dark
Harbour
Road

776

Fundy Coast

Money Cove Loop, Eel Lake Trail

views across the bay. In clear weather there is a spectacular view from Big Head back in a southerly direction towards Hay Point. The level trail continues through wet corduroy sections of Gordon Heath and later Bog Heath. There are a number of good views across the bay. Pass behind a red cottage and turn inland on a wider track used by four-wheelers. There are several wet spots, followed by a boggy section. At one point, you pass a higher elevation on the left of the trail. The path swings away from the coast, keeps straight at a fork, and soon reaches the coast again. When you come to a sign saying "To Seal Cove" pointing towards the right, you have reached Sloop Cove. A short spur to the left leads to a lookout, and the main trail continues straight. Just beyond, there is another turnoff to the left (leading to a cabin); again, continue straight. The trail starts to descend and then turns off to the left at a 90 degree angle just before reaching a large field. Soon after, the trail turns inland (right), crosses a small pond on two corduroy bridges, and continues to a signpost near Dwellys Cove at 12 km (7.5 mi).

Section 3: DWELLYS COVE TO LITTLE DARK HARBOUR. At the signpost, continue straight toward Dark Harbour. The path descends fairly steeply. In this area, orange marking tape indicates the trail. Grassy areas alternate with woods. At one point, the trail swings off to the left just before it appears to fizzle out. Turn left at a T-junction. Soon after, the trail swings to the right and continues until it reaches the cliffs at a lookout from which Little Dark Harbour may be seen on the far right. The trail parallels the cliffs, which are extremely high in this area. The path then descends to a brook, crosses it, and passes through a pretty field with ferns. Follow the wide tracks that lead inland. The trail dips down to a brook, ascends again and is joined by wide, grassy tracks from the right. The trail then descends steeply for a short distance and reaches a brook at 14 km (8.7 mi).

Section 4: LITTLE DARK HARBOUR TO DARK HARBOUR. From the brook, the trail ascends again. Keep left at a fork. As the trail levels off and swings to the right, there is a fine view back towards Little Dark Harbour with its pebble beach and steep ravine. Pass a white cabin at a field and enter the woods parallel to the coast next to the house. Red marks on trees and rocks mark the trail. The path continues through the woods parallel to the coast, but in this area there are no more views of the coast. The trail turns inland and descends at Herring Cove, passes a lookout, crosses a brook, and continues on its inland direction before turning back to the coast. Bear left at the sign pointing to Dark Harbour. After passing a lookout, the path goes up and down, passes an old shack, and continues straight at a turnoff. Soon it reaches the Western Head Lookout, which is truly spectacular. Western Head looks out over Dark Harbour with its salmon pens, small boats, and cabins. At a T-junction, the trail turns sharply to the left. At a fork, keep left to reach lookout #1 with another fine view of Dark Harbour. The rooty main trail takes the right fork and starts to descend. At the bottom, it crosses a brook on the "Wet Sock Bridge," built by a Scout troop, and climbs fairly steeply though a logged-over area to a parking lot on Dark Harbour Road at 18.4 km (11.4 mi). turn left onto the paved road for 0.9 km (0.6 mi) to the continuation of the trail towards The Whistle.

Section 5: DARK HARBOUR TO THE WHISTLE. The trail continues at a sign pointing towards The Whistle on the north side of Dark Harbour Road. The trail passes a number of cabins, then it narrows, and, just before reaching a red cabin, turns off to the right. A steep ascent follows to the top of the hill, where the path turns left. It closely follows the edge of a steep slope that soon turns into a cliff. There are some spectacular views of Dark Harbour as well as of the coast of Maine and Campobello Island.

The trail leads through softwoods before it descends into a ravine. It crosses a brook and then ascends again and continues along the edge of the cliffs. On the plateau, the path goes through nice hay-scented ferns before it starts to descend again. Cross a logged-over area and keep left at a junction. (The blue-blazed trail that joins our path is the southern part of Money Cove Loop; see directions on page 95.) Cross the edge of a beaver pond, and soon you reach The Crossing, a 4-way junction, at 22.9 km (14.2 mi).

Here the blue-blazed trail to the left leads down to Money Cove Beach (see the trail description on page 96), and the woods road to the right eventually joins the northern part of Money Cove Loop. Follow the red discs straight uphill and bear to the left at a somewhat inconspicuous fork. (The yellow-blazed right fork is the northern half of the Money Cove Loop.) The rocky trail soon reaches a plateau with a nice view. The trail continues through hay-scented fern fields along the edge of the cliffs with excellent lookouts from clifftops. Back in the woods, the path reaches "The Signpost," another 4-way junction, at 25.2 km (15.7 mi). (The left spur descends steeply to Indian Beach, and the right trail goes to Eel Lake; see the trail description on page 98). Continue straight, and after a short distance there are some views of the lighthouse at the northernmost tip of Grand Manan. A rocky descent is followed by pleasant hiking on a level, grassy trail. Turn left directly behind a powerline and follow it to the paved road. Turn right and follow the road to the Long Eddy Lightstation, locally called The Whistle, at 27.2 km (16.9 mi).

Section 6: THE WHISTLE TO WHALE COVE. The trail continues to the right of the Long Eddy Lightstation next to a traffic sign, where the road makes a 90 degree turn. The narrow path first ascends and as it levels off there are some good views of the coastline. After a steep and rooty climb you reach the site of a 1985 fire at Ashburton Head. Looking back, you have a nice view down to The Bishop rock formation. The trail swings inland and continues to the end of a gravel road. Follow the grassy woods road and turn left to Eel Brook Beach and Whale Cove. The path descends and crosses Eel Brook via some logs, then climbs again. Turn left at a T-junction (turning right leads to a dump, where crows and seagulls congregate).

The trail is level for a while, and at 29.8 km (18.5 mi), it forks. The left fork leads to Eel Brook Beach. The main trail keeps to the right and ascends through softwoods along the edge of the cliff. The path then passes a new building and keeps close to the cliff with spectacular views across to Ashburton Head, Seven Days Work and a herring weir. At a junction with a dirt road, turn right, and at a 4-way junction, continue straight and follow a grassy woods road until the red-blazed trail turns left to Whale Cove. The Whale Cove boat launch is reached at 32.3 km (20.1 mi). Walk along the pebble beach for some 500 m/yds to the end of Cemetrey Road and the continuation of the trail towards Swallowtail Lighthouse. The small turnaround at the end of Cemetrey Road (a narrow dirt road, which is also called Church Road) is reached at 32.8 km (20.4 mi).

Section 7: WHALE COVE TO SWALLOWTAIL LIGHTHOUSE. Where the Cemetery Road ends at Whale Cove, the red-blazed trail continues along the coastline. At 33.8 km (21 mi), a lookout allows an excellent view of Whale Cove and the Hole-in-the-Wall formation. The trail continues in an easterly direction with a few good views of The Hole. As the path swings inland, it reaches a junction that could easily be missed. The wide trail straight ahead leads to an old airfield. On the extreme left, the path continues towards Fish Head and the Swallowtail Lighthouse.

Fish Head consists of an ancient pipestone quarry, a bonsai forest along the cliffs and some nice views. From here, the trail turns south and follows the edge of the cliff. There are more spectacular views in the region. Watch for the blazes; just as the path gets wider and turns inland towards the old airfield, the trail swings to the left and continues along the coast. From time to time, the Swallowtail Lighthouse is visible.

The trail turns inland for a short distance, and, just before it reaches a dirt road, it turns left and reaches a lookout and picnic table. From here, the path continues straight, then keeps to the left at a sign saying "Orange Trail to HITW Park Entrance" (Hole-in-the-Wall), and comes to the Barite Mine site. Soon after, turn right onto a gravel road and right again to a paved road. At 36.4 km (22.6 mi), you arrive at the Swallowtail Lighthouse.

Trail Features: This coastal trail leads from the southernmost lighthouse via the northernmost lighthouse to the picturesque Swallowtail Lighthouse. It passes by such idyllic places as Hay Point and the southwest coast as well as Hole-in-the-Wall on the northeastern coast.

MONEY COVE LOOP

Length: 13.8 km (8.6 mi) [+ 0.5 km (0.3 mi) side trail to Quigley Hill]
Type: loop
Difficulty: moderate
Ascent: 130 m (430 ft)

Hiking Time: 4 hrs [+ 20 min rtn]
Map: 21 B/15 Campobello Island
Trail Condition: wet spots

Access: From the North Head ferry terminal, follow Highway 776 for 1.4 km (0.9 mi) and turn right onto Whistle Road. Follow this road for 500 m/yd, then turn left into the North Head Community Park and Playground. There is parking for up to 10 vehicles. The trailhead is located at the far right of the grounds.

Trail Markings: The trail is marked by yellow and blue metal discs on trees. With one exception (pointed out below) the trail is easy to follow.

The Trail: The wide trail ascends gently. Ignore some smaller side trails departing to the right. At 0.7 km (0.4 mi), the trail joins a woods road and continues to the right. Some 300 m/yd ahead, a smaller trail departs to the right; this is where the trail will return later. Continue straight, following the blue blazes. Another short distance ahead, turn right at a fork. The trail to Money Cove continues to climb a gentle grade, crosses a power line and reaches a rocky plateau. Bear to the left.

There are a few wet spots on the mostly grassy trail. The level trail leads through mixed woods and gets drier. At 3.1 km (1.9 mi), the trail reaches a small rocky plateau. The view from here is limited by young growth. The trail descends to the left; a rope has been installed to guide hikers down the steep descent. Just as you reach the bottom, turn right and keep below the steep hills on the right. After a short distance, the trail turns left at a 90-degree angle. The path is partially obscured in this area; watch for blue marking tape. At 4 km (2.5 mi) you reach a beaver pond. Cross via some logs on the right at the drainage, and shortly beyond turn right into the woods. Cross an old woods road and continue straight through mixed forest. After some distance, the trail is joined by a wide trail on the left. A sometime pond is visible on the right.

Towards the end of a logged-over area there is a fork; here the Money Cove Loop joins the Lighthouse Trail, which is marked by red discs. Turn right (the left leads to Dark Harbour), cross a brook, and soon you reach a 4-way junction known as "The Crossing." To the left, a 40-minute (return) spur leads to Money Cove. (This is a very worthwhile side trail that gives access to the beach. It is marked by blue blazes and red discs. The trail is level at first, but it becomes gradually steeper before ending at a rocky pebble beach next to a steep ravine.) At "The Crossing," the trail to the right is marked by a yellow blaze. It is, however, NOT the return trail but an uninteresting wide woods road that eventually joins up with our loop. Follow the trail straight ahead. As it climbs, the trail forks; while the red-blazed left fork continues the Lighthouse Trail along the coast, the loop trail follows the yellow-blazed right fork that leads into the woods. There are some signs referring to this trail as the "North Trail," which also follows a northerly direction towards North Head.

The trail soon levels off and hiking along the woods road is good. At 7.4 km (4.6 mi), this trail is joined by another trail on the right. Turn sharply to the right here and the yellow blazes. Continue straight at a fork and pass Little Eel Lake, keeping it to the left. The trail ascends in a wet area and leads into the woods. At 9.6 km

(6 mi), a side trail to Quigley Hill departs from the main trail to the right. This yellow-blazed 20 minute (return) side trail allows some views towards the Sydney Hill, opposite.

Return to the main trail and turn right to continue along the level path. It leads through an open area with scattered birch trees. Continue straight at a 4-way junction. Soon, the trail crosses under power lines, turns right, and descends. Keep right at a fork and bear to the left as the trail joins the familiar wide woods road at 12.8 km (8 mi). Shortly after, turn left onto a smaller side trail which returns to the trailhead.

Trail Features: A nice trail through mostly mixed woods where the work of the beaver can be observed at several points. The ponds provide good opportunities to watch big game. The side trail to Money Cove will give the hiker access to the bay and the rugged western coast.

EEL LAKE TRAIL

Length: 7.2 km (4.4 mi) rtn	**Hiking Time:** 2 hrs 30 min rtn
Type: linear	**Map:** 21 B/15 Campobello Island
Difficulty: moderate	
Ascent: 100 m (300 ft)	**Trail Condition:** dry, rooty

Access: From the ferry terminal, turn left onto Highway 776. As the highway makes a 90-degree turn to the left, turn right onto Whistle Road. Follow it for 2.7 km (1.7 mi); the trail is located on the left side of the road. Take the left of the two adjacent dirt roads for 0.6 km (0.4 mi) to a parking area on the right side of the road.

Trail Markings: The trail is marked by light-blue paint blazes and blue metal discs. Without a guide, it is easy to get lost on this trail.

The Trail: As indicated by a blue metal disc, follow the power lines. As they turn to the right (north), the trail departs to the left. It soon crosses Eel Brook on a wooden bridge. At the signpost "Indian Beach," keep right and watch carefully for the markers. Turn left at a junction and continue in the same direction. At 1.1 km (0.7 mi), turn again to the left. About 300 m/yd beyond, take the right fork at a junction and hike on the wide tracks for a while. After 2 km (1.2 mi), keep right at the next junction. The trail leads through beautiful fields of the hay-scented fern that is so characteristic of Grand Manan. Continue straight at the next junction (the left path leads to a cabin). For a short stretch there are no blazes, but Eel Lake becomes visible on the left. At a small fenced-in enclosure, turn off to the right up a small hill. This turnoff is easily missed.

From here on, the trail is easy to find. At a sign saying "Indian Beach" and "North Head," turn left through fern fields. Turn left again on the now rocky and rooty woods road and cross a small brook. The trail descends gently, ascends again, then leads through mature woods to the "Signpost" at 3.2 km (2 mi). At this point, this trail connects with the Lighthouse Trail.

A short spur continues straight ahead and descends steeply to a pebble beach and lagoon at Indian Beach.

Trail Features: A walk through mature forest, several open spaces filled with hay-scented ferns, and access to Eel Lake, which is thought to be the crater of an extinct volcano. The trail also gives access to the northwestern coast at Indian Beach.

FLOCK OF SHEEP TRAIL

Length: 6 km (3.8 mi) rtn
Difficulty: easy to moderate
Hiking Time: 2 hrs 30 min rtn

Type: linear
Ascent: 45 m (150 ft)
Map: 21 B/10 Grand Manan
Trail Condition: dry

Access: From the ferry terminal, follow Highway 776 south for about 29 km (18 mi) to its end at the Southwest Head Lighthouse. About six vehicles can park here. The trailhead is located just south of the foghorn next to the fence.

Trail Markings: The trail is marked by red metal discs.

The Trail: Walk south from the parking lot and take the narrow path across the heath. The trail continues through softwoods. At one point, the path turns right onto a driveway towards "Bear's Den," but before reaching this house, it turns left into the woods. Walk parallel to the coastline and you reach the Lower Flock of Sheep, named for a number of round, whitish boulders transported here during the last ice age. Fishermen likened them to a flock of sheep when seen from the sea. The trail continues along the cliffs and reaches the Upper Flock of Sheep. The path soon turns right onto a dirt road, and immediately left again towards Pats Cove. Walk on the flat rock shelf, caused by glacial movement, until you reach Pats Cove and a turnaround. From here, you can either return on the same trail or via the road — a 2.1 km (1.3 mi) walk.

Trail Features: The main features of this trail are the white rounded granite boulders and the impressive views from the edges of the cliffs along the trail. The Smith family has kindly put up benches for everyone to savour the view. Treat their property with care, and enjoy!

RED POINT TRAIL

Length: 3 km (1.9 mi) rtn **Hiking Time:** 1 hr rtn
Type: linear   **Map:** 21 B/10 Grand
Difficulty: easy   Manan
Ascent: negligible   **Trail Condition:** dry,
                                mostly boardwalk

Access: From the ferry terminal, follow Highway 776 south towards Anchorage Provincial Park. About 3.2 km (2 mi) before you reach Seal Cove, turn left towards the provincial park. Bear left at a fork (the right leads to the campground) and continue for 0.7 km (0.4 mi) to a T-junction. Turn right and continue a short distance to a parking lot with roofed picnic area and the trailhead.

Trail Markings: The trail is marked by orange plastic blazes, but it is easy to follow.

The Trail: This nature walk with interpretive signs starts as a level footpath through alders. The trail skirts the coast. A short side trail to the right leads to the Anchorage Provincial Park campground. Continue straight through mixed woods. Benches provide moments of relaxation at some nice lookouts. When the trail leaves the woods, it enters a stand of medium-sized and smaller alder bushes. The trail leads through a small gate and soon ends at a turnaround next to a dirt road.

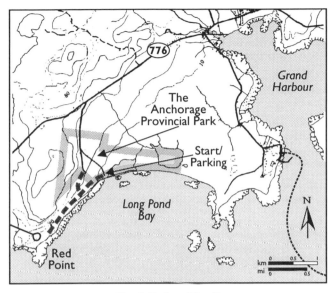

Red Point Trail

Trail Features: The key features of this trail are the fine views across the bay to Wood Island. Also visible at the end of the trail in the vicinity of Red Point at the shore are the two main geological formations composing Grand Manan Island: the red sedimentary rock and the younger, grey volcanic rock.

BEECH HILL TRAIL

Length: 1 km (0.6 mi) rtn
Type: linear
Difficulty: easy
Ascent: 40 m (130 ft)
Hiking Time: 15 min rtn
Map: 21 B/10 Grand Manan
Trail Condition: some wet spots

Access: From the ferry terminal, follow Highway 776 south for 6 km (3.7 mi). Turn right towards Dark Harbour and the airport. After 1.3 km (0.8 mi), at a fork, continue straight towards Grand Harbour. After 700 m/yd, a cemetrey is located on the left side of the road. About 1.1 km (0.7 mi) beyond the graveyard, there is a woods road on the right side of the road. Drive up this road for a short distance and park at a designated place where the trail turns off to the right.

Trail Markings: There are some red discs, but once the trailhead is found, the trail is easy to follow.

The Trail: Follow an old woods road to a small clearing. The trail turns right and leads at first through mixed forest. It soon reaches an old clearing with young growth. From here, the trail ascends and reaches a small platform on rocky ground. This is the top of Beech Hill; it offers excellent views towards the east.

Trail Features: The fine view from the summit of Beech Hill towards North Head, Grand Harbour, the islands and part of the inland makes this short trail worthwhile.

SUNBURY SHORES NATURE TRAIL

Length: 0.8 km (0.5 mi)   **Hiking Time:** 15 min
Type: loop   **Map:** 21 G/3 St. Stephen
Difficulty: easy   **Trail Condition:** dry
Ascent: negligible

Access: From downtown St. Andrews, take Water Street in a northwesterly direction (keep the waterfront to your left). The trailhead is located 250 m/yds beyond

Charles Street on the right. Next to the trailhead, there is parking for only two vehicles.

Trail Markings: The trail is clearly marked throughout.

Trail Features: Brochures outlining the features of this self-guiding trail may be available at the trailhead during the summer months. This trail is particularly beautiful in the spring when the apple and cherry trees are in full bloom. The trail is maintained by the Sunbury Shores Arts and Nature Centre.

NEW RIVER BEACH TRAIL
(New River Beach Provincial Park)

Length: 5 km (3.1 mi)
Type: loop
Difficulty: easy
Ascent: negligible

Hiking Time: 1 hr 30 min
Map: 21 G/2 St. George
(and provincial tourism publication, 1-800-561-0123)
Trail Condition: generally dry, wet spots at tip of peninsula and bog, long boardwalk.

Access: From Saint John, take Highway 1 west for about 55 km (35 mi) from the city limits. Turn left to the New River Beach Provincial Park, which is located to the left of the highway at the Bay of Fundy. Pass a spur road to a campsite and go straight, then take the right fork. The road ends at a large parking area. The trailhead is located at the far left of the parking lot, close to a small cove.

Trail Markings: None, but the trail is obvious.

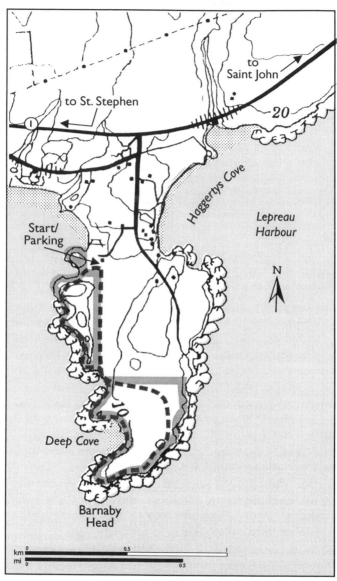

to Saint John

to St. Stephen

20

Haggertys Cove

Lepreau
Harbour

Start/
Parking

N

Deep Cove

Barnaby
Head

km 0   0.5   1
mi 0   0.5

New River Beach Trail

The Trail: At the small beach, which is called Tommys Cove, turn left. The herring weir you see is an efficient method of catching fish that has a long history. Walk across a little footbridge and then turn left again. At this point there is a sign and the beginning of a lengthy boardwalk that makes up most of the first half of the trail. The trail leads a short distance through the woods before passing Raspberry Cove and later Deadmans Cove. The latter has a lovely sandy beach and ends at a rocky peninsula. Continue to gravelly Chitticks Beach (named after an Irish settler of the 1800s) where the trail reaches a meadow and the remains of an old homestead. The trail continues to skirt the Bay of Fundy. Keep right at a fork and follow the trail along the rugged coast. (The trail will later return to the fork.)

At a sign at Deep Cove, continue straight ahead; the trail to the left is a shortcut leading to a bog. At Barnaby Head, a bell buoy can be heard that warns skippers of the dangerous waters. Beyond Barnaby Head the trail continues parallel to the coast, with some very short side trails leading to spectacular lookouts at sheer cliffs. The main trail is frequently wet in this area. As soon as the trail turns inland, the terrain opens up. The vegetation is no longer that of a windswept coastal forest but that of a bog. The trail continues through the forest, with a spur to the left connecting it to the coast. Back at the clearing at Chitticks Beach, the trail continues straight past the sign. At one point there is a short but wide boardwalk to the right, which leads to a lookout overlooking another bog. Continue straight across a tiny covered bridge. The trail ends at a small bridge near the parking lot.

Trail Features: The main features of this trail are the spectacular coastline and the bog vegetation. The coastline is particularly interesting with its shore life –

Sign at New River Beach. H.A. EISELT

barnacles, sea urchins, rock crabs, and sand dollars – and its views. These alone make this trail worthwhile. The other attraction, the bog, is unique with its dwarf conifers, insect-eating pitcher plants, sundews and Labrador tea. A trail guide describing the features of the trail in more detail is available from Tourism New Brunswick.

TAYLOR ISLAND PERIMETER TRAIL

(Irving Nature Park, Irving Co.)

Length: 6.3 km (4 mi)   **Hiking Time:** 2 hrs 15 min
Type: loop   **Map:** 21 G/1 Musquash,
Difficulty: easy   leaflets available at park
Ascent: negligible   **Trail Condition:** very well
maintained

Access: Approaching Saint John from the west on Highway 1, take exit 107A to the Reversing Falls. Turn right at the Stop sign onto Bleury for 0.5 km (0.3 mi), and turn right again at a Stop sign onto Sand Cove Road. Follow this road for 3.2 km (2 mi) until the pavement ends. Here a sign welcomes visitors to the Irving Nature Park. Continue on the dirt road for another 0.8 km (0.5 mi) where the road forks and starts to ascend. Continue for another 0.6 km (0.4 mi) to a fork. Turn left into a parking lot just above an information pavilion. From here, walk up a few wooden steps to another parking lot. The trail starts on the far right, next to the cliff.

Trail Markings: None, but for the most part the trail is obvious.

The Trail: The trail parallels the rocky coast of the Bay of Fundy and the gravel road; note the herring weir. At an outcrop, there are some short spur trails; keep to the right. The trail continues along the peninsula and looks out over the beach far below the cliff. The footpath winds along the cliffs until at 2.7 km (1.7 mi) it reaches the southwestern tip of Taylor Island, where a nice lookout provides views of the bay and the rock formation called The Gorge.

From here, the trail rounds the peninsula, and the cliffs are no longer so steep. Keep left at a fork. When the trail reaches a road, turn left and walk along the beach. Towards the end of the beach, just before it reaches a stand of craggy black spruce, the trail turns inland at a right angle. Before the trail reaches the road again, it turns off to the left. The trail continues along the coast, passes a beach and later, mudflats, where shore birds stop to feed during the fall migration.

At a T-junction, the trail first continues a few steps to the right and then swings left again in the original direction. The path now leaves the conifers and heads into a stand of alder bushes. At a fork, the right trail leads to the main parking lot ("Squirrel Trail"), whereas the island perimetre trail continues to the left. At 5.8 km (3.6 mi), a boardwalk departs to the left into the Saints Rest Marsh.

Continuing straight, the path reaches a fork, where it turns to the right. The trail ascends, crosses the main dirt road, soon crosses another road and heads into the woods. There is a maze of trails in this area, so it is best to keep left near the cliffs. After a short distance, the trail reaches the upper parking lot and completes the loop.

Trail Features: The park is a donation of the late K.C. Irving to the people of New Brunswick. Opened to the public in June 1992, it has proved a very successful recreation site for New Brunswickers. The main attraction of this trail is the variety of different ecosystems it includes, ranging from the rugged Fundy Coast to tidal mudflats and a marsh. Of particular interest is the spur trail into the Saints Rest Marsh, which contains marram beach grass and frequent visits by great blue herons, black ducks and greater yellowlegs. The trail is very well maintained with bridges and boardwalk sections across muddy parts. The park is open during daylight hours.

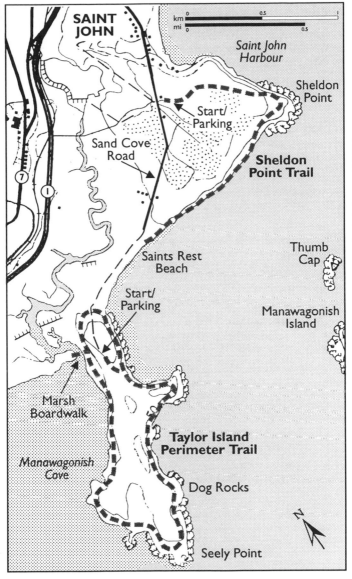

Sheldon Point & Taylor Island Perimeter Trails

Sheldon Point Trail

(Irving Nature Park, Irving Co.)

Length: 8 km (5 mi) rtn	**Hiking Time:** 2 hrs rtn
Type: linear	**Map:** 21 G/1 Musquash
Difficulty: easy to moderate	**Trail Condition:** some slippery spots
Ascent: negligible	

Access: Entering Saint John from the west on Highway 1, take exit 107A to the Reversing Falls. Turn right at the Stop sign onto Bleury, and, after 0.5 km (0.3 mi), turn right again at the Stop sign onto Sand Cove Road. Follow this road for 1.7 km (1.1 mi). On the left side of the road is a sign saying "Irving Nature Park." There is parking here for about 20 vehicles. The trailhead is located at the far end of the lot next to a big barn. *Note:* The gates of the parking lot are locked between 8 p.m. and 8 a.m., and bikes and ATVs are not allowed on the trail.

Trail Markings: There are occasional wooden signs with green arrows, but the trail is obvious and cannot be missed.

The Trail: The wide, gravelly trail descends from the barn, turns right, and leads into the woods where it soon gets narrower. The path continues high above the Fundy coast through mixed woods. Note the herring weir in the bay. At about the halfway mark, the trail enters an open field at Sheldon Point. The rocky cliffs and the coves down below are very spectacular in this area. Beyond this point, the trail soon leads down to the beach.

At the beach, turn right and continue along the sandy cliffs and the bay to the end of the trail at a parking lot. This part of the trail may be impassable during exceptionally high tides. From the trail end, you can either retrace your steps or turn right onto the paved road and return to the parking lot. The latter option is considerably shorter but nowhere near as pleasant as the former.

Trail Features: The trail features the diversity of the Fundy coastline from rugged cliffs to a sandy beach and offers spectacular panoramic views.

ROCKWOOD PARK LOOP

Length: 8.6 km (5.3 mi) rtn
Type: loop
Difficulty: easy to moderate
Ascent: negligible

Hiking Time: 2 hrs 15 min
Map: 21 G/8 Saint John and Rockwood Park guide
Trail Condition: wet spots off the main trail

Access: Rockwood Park is located in the city of Saint John. You can reach it by following Union Street in an easterly direction. Turn left onto Crown Street just behind CHSJ radio and TV station. Cross the bridge over Highway 1 and continue straight through some traffic lights, at which point the street is called Mt. Pleasant Road. Turn right at the sign saying "Welcome to Rockwood Park." At the end of Lily Lake, cross a dam to the left and continue for 0.8 km (0.5 mi) to a parking lot. The trail starts on the right side of the parking lot at a gate.

Trail Markings: The trail is unmarked but easy to follow.

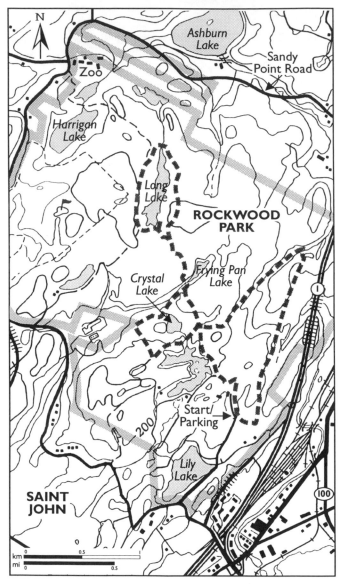

Rockwood Park Loop

The Trail: Pass through the gate and follow a wide woods road. Keep to the left at a sharp bend, and keep to the left again when you reach a grassy area. When the trail passes under some power lines, a nearby highway can be heard. The trail leads again beneath some power lines and starts to ascend fairly steeply. Turn around, catch your breath, and enjoy the nice view of Westmoreland Heights!

At 2.4 km (1.5 mi), you reach a T-junction. Turn right onto another gravelly woods road. Note Crystal Lake far below on the left. After a little while, the trail reaches the tip of Frying Pan Lake. Continue on the wide trail, pass a small trail that turns off to the right, and turn off onto the next small path to the right, which leaves the wide trail next to two big rocks. The path is grassy and leads through dense cedars. Continue on the path after it is joined from the left by another narrow path and continue straight as a path departs to the right. The path swings to the left and leads through some wet spots, some with cattails. Cross a wooden bridge at the head of Long Lake and continue on the path, which soon reaches a T-junction at a wide trail. Turn left and follow the trail to Long Lake on the left. (Turning right at this point would lead you to the Cherry Brook Zoo.)

Just beyond the lake, we suggest you take a short spur to the left along the lake. The narrow path leads to a rock overlooking the lake. This very scenic spot invites hikers to rest and relax. Back on the main trail, continue to the left. Pass Frying Pan Lake again, and, just before the trail crosses under some power lines, turn right onto a narrow path. The path follows the power lines; note Crystal Lake to the left of the trail. As some greenhouses come into view, the path turns sharply to the left. Continue along the often muddy trail to a T-junction and turn to the left. At some point the Fisher Lakes becomes visible on the right side of the trail. At another T-junction ("The Pla-

Feeding the ducks at Rockwood Park. H.A. EISELT

teau"), turn right onto the paved road. Keep left and walk on the road. Note the Fisher Lakes on the right with the huge boulders, remnants of the last ice age. At some point a small path on the left side of the road provides an alternative for the last short distance to the parking lot.

Trail Features: This 880-hectare (2,200-acre) park is a quiet retreat from the city; only the sound of an occasional siren from the ambulances at the hospital reminds the hiker of the closeness of urban Saint John. The city has received an award for the design of Rockwood Park. The trail provides some fine views of lakes, peninsulas and rocks shaped by glaciation. At the trailhead, there is a children's animal farm. Cherry Brook Zoo is located at the other side of the park. In season, brochures with details are available at the park or yearround from Parks Department, Saint John, N.B. For more information, call (506) 658-2829.

HAMMOND RIVER NATURE TRAIL

Length: 1.7 km (1.1 mi)
Type: loop
Difficulty: easy to moderate
Ascent: 70 m (200 ft)

Hiking Time: 45 min
Map: 21 H/5 Loch Lomond, trail map at log cabin
Trail Condition: dry

Access: From Saint John, take Highway 1 east. Take exit 131 just past a trailer park, and follow Highway 100 for 3.8 km (2.4 mi). Just beyond a lawn ornament store, turn left onto Hammond River Road. Follow this road for 3.4 km (2.1 mi), crossing the railway tracks on the way. At a Stop sign, take the right fork onto Neck Road and follow it for 0.8 km (0.5 mi). Turn right onto Raynar Drive, and after 400 m/yd the entrance to the park is on the right side of the street. The short access road ends at a parking lot next to a log cabin. The trailhead is located to the right of the log cabin.

Trail Markings: All trails in the park are well marked and cannot be missed.

The Trail: The trail first leads through some softwoods. After about 100 m/yd, it turns off to the left and descends rather steeply. (A short side trail continues straight ahead to South Lookout, from which Darlings Island can be seen.) At this point, follow the signs saying "South." When the trail swings to the left, follow the signs saying "Lowland." This part of the path parallels the Hammond River and allows some good views. Beyond an observation deck, the trail swings sharply to the left and starts to ascend; follow the signs saying "North." The trail ends at the back of the log cabin.

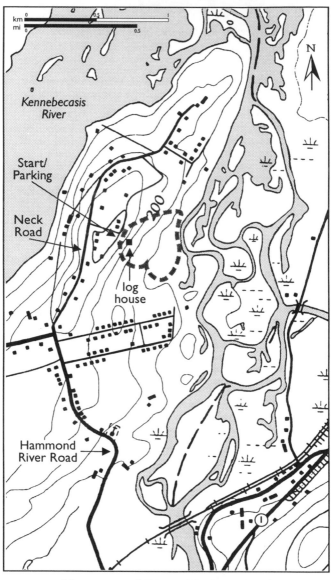

km 0   0.5   1
mi 0   0.5

Kennebecasis
River

Start/
Parking

Neck
Road

log
house

Hammond
River Road

N

Hammond River Nature Trail

Trail Features: The park received a major face-lift in 1991 and is now well marked and much improved in general. The nature trail passes a number of interesting sights, ranging from old apple orchards to nurse logs and a kame (a glacial feature). The log cabin at the trailhead houses a visitor centre, open daily from 9 a.m. to 5 p.m. from the end of May to August. A brochure describing the many side trails and features of the park is available at the log cabin. To receive a copy of the brochure, write to the Town of Quispamsis, Quispamsis, N.B. E0G 2W0 or call the log cabin at (506) 849-4529 or the town office at (506) 847-8878.

FUNDY FOOTPATH
(in 6 sections)

Length: 25.7 km (16 mi) one way
Type: linear
Difficulty: strenuous
Ascent: 200m (650ft); 1600m (5300 ft) cumulative
Hiking Time: 2-3 days one way

Map: 21 H/11 Waterford and 21 H/6 Salmon River. For the very useful Fundy Model Forest Trail Map, call (506) 856 2322 (Geographic Information Corporation)
Trail Condition: rocky, rooty, wet areas, some sections can only be hiked at low tide

Summary:

Section 1: 2.5 km (1.5 mi)
Section 2: 4.6 km (2.9 mi)
Section 3: 5.7 km (3.5 mi)
Hiking time for sections 1 to 3: 1 to 2 days, depending on the tides

Section 4: 4.5 km (2.8 mi)
Section 5: 1.9 km (1.2 mi)
Section 6: 6.5 km (4 mi)
Hiking time for sections 4 to 6: 1 day
The entire trail: 25.7 km (16 mi), 2 to 3 days,
    depending on the tides

Access: (1) TO THE TRAILHEAD EAST. The Fundy Footpath
starts at Goose River at the Southwestern boundary of
Fundy National Park. To reach the footpath, hike the
Goose River Trail to the beach. At low tide, turn right at
the beach and cross Rossiter Brook. Keep left and skirt
the east bank of Goose River. The trailhead of the
Fundy Footpath is located just above an old logging
dam on the west bank of Goose River. Eventually, the
Goose River Trail will connect with the Fundy Footpath
via the National Trail, which leads from the trailhead of
the Fundy Footpath via Rossiter Brook to some point
on the Goose River Trail. The advantage of the National Trail connector will be that it can be hiked
regardless of the tides. For further information, call Edwin Melanson at (506) 855-5089 or Alonzo Legere at
(506) 386-2867.

(2) TO THE TRAILHEAD WEST. The trail ends at Dustan
Brook and climbs out on a side trail to the Little
Salmon River Road. To reach the trail end by car, take
Highway 121 in an easterly direction through down-
town Sussex. Cross the stone bridge, and at a junction
with Highway 111, bear to the right onto Waterford
Road towards St. Martins. After a short distance, High-
way 111 turns off to the right; continue straight on
Waterford Road for 11.8 km (7.3 mi) to a fork. Bear left
and cross underneath a bridge, following the sign to
Martin Head. After some 400 m/yds, continue straight,
ignoring the wider road that swings to the left. Soon

the paved road becomes a good gravel road. Stay on this gravel road, pass by Walton Lake, and, 4 km (2.5 mi) later, pass by Crawford Lake with its many cottages. Soon after, you reach a junction with the Old Shepody Road. Continue straight, pass Grassy Lake on the right of the road, and bear to the left at a fork. A short distance later, cross Little Salmon River on a small wooden bridge. At 1.7 km (1.1 mi) past the bridge, the Little Salmon River Road turns off to the right. On the far left side of the road there are two white and green blazes on two birch trees. This dirt road is rougher and narrower, but manageable with a passenger vehicle. At a fork 3.5 km (2.2 mi) along the Little Salmon River Road, keep to the right, and at another fork a short distance farther, keep again to the right. About 6 km (3.7 mi) along Little Salmon River Road, there is a turnoff to the right. Keep straight here, and continue for another 2 km (1.2 mi) to the yellow-blazed side trail of the Fundy Footpath where the road turns left at a 90-degree angle.

Trail Markings: The trail is blazed by white 2" x 6" paint blazes (do not mistake the blazes with whitish lichens on trees!) Access trails are marked in yellow, and campsites are blazed in blue. The blazes are clearly visible throughout. Distances at intervals of 1 km (0.6 mi) are indicated by trees marked with two green bands. Changes in direction are indicated by two paint blazes, one underneath the other. At this time there is still a significant amount of orange and blue marking tape at and near the trail. The tape was used by those who built and blazed the trail, in part as temporary markings of the new trail but also to mark the access routes for the trail builders. If not specifically mentioned, marking tape should be ignored as it does not always coincide with the trail.

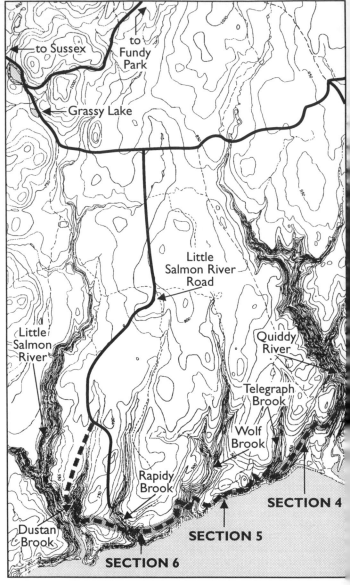

to Sussex

to Fundy Park

Grassy Lake

Little Salmon River Road

Little Salmon River

Quiddy River

Telegraph Brook

Wolf Brook

Rapidy Brook

SECTION 4

SECTION 5

Dustan Brook

SECTION 6

Fundy

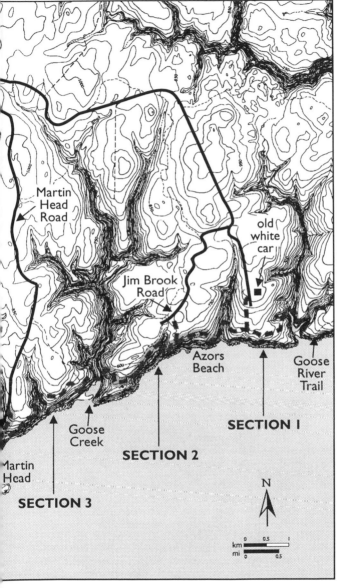

Martin
Head
Road

old
white
car

Jim Brook
Road

Azors
Beach

Goose
River
Trail

SECTION 1

Goose
Creek

SECTION 2

Martin
Head

SECTION 3

N

km
mi

ootpath

The Trail:

Section 1: GOOSE RIVER TO AZORS BEACH. At the west bank of Goose River, about 20 m/yds above the old logging dam at a cairn, the white-blazed Fundy Footpath leads into the woods. It climbs immediately, crosses a small brook and ascends in several switchbacks to reach a plateau after some 300 m/yds. The narrow path leads through small wildflower meadows and young growth, swings sharply to the left, then swings to the left again. It continues through an open wet area, passes the 1 km sign, and goes into the woods shortly after. Just before the trail enters the woods, a short, boggy side trail to the left leads to a meadow overlooking Martin Head. (The side trail is marked with some orange and yellow marking tape.) The main trail enters the woods, descends, crosses a brook, and at 1.7 km (1 mi) reaches the junction with the short spur to the Primrose wilderness campground and the White Car access trail. (This access trail climbs some 600 m/yds to the exit road at the wreck of a white car, hence its name.) At the junction, the Fundy Footpath continues in a westerly direction, dips down to a small dry brook, crosses an old logging road and leads through mossy mixed forest. The trail then starts to descend steeply and finally levels off at Rose Brook, which soon leads to Azors Beach. Follow the brook to the left towards the beach, where white paint blazes on rocks mark the trail. Shortly before the trail reaches the beach, it ascends steeply to the right (see Section 2). From the beach you can see the steep cliffs and the Martin Head Peninsula.

Section 2: AZORS BEACH TO GOOSE CREEK. The trail follows Rose Brook, and, a short distance before reaching Azors Beach, it steeply climbs the western side of the brook. There are a few muddy spots on the way up. As the path ascends, bear to the right at an inconspicuous fork. The trail crosses a tiny brook at 2.9 km (1.8 mi). It continues to climb, but at a gentler grade. There are some views of the bay through the trees. Crossing two small, dry brooks, the trail goes up and down. The trail then crosses a claim line with red markings and follows a ridge with a steep decline on its left. The trail stays high, allowing frequent views of the bay. At 4.1 km (4.5 mi), an exit trail on the left departs to the old Vernon Goldmine and the Jim Brook Road. The trail now starts to descend gradually while leading away from the coast. It crosses Jim Brook and ascends again steeply to a beautiful hardwood grove. After crossing another small creek at 5.2 km (3.2 mi), the trail turns sharply to the left; this bend is easily missed. The path crosses a small ravine and passes some sinkholes to the left and right. There are a number of deep holes next to the trail, so caution is advised. At one point there is a very impressive gap to the left, allowing farther views onto the bay. The trail starts to descend steeply and crosses two gullies, and then it starts to descend in earnest while turning away from the coast. The descent ends at 7.1 km (4.4 mi) at Goose Creek.

Section 3: GOOSE CREEK TO MARTIN HEAD. If the tide is low, continuing the Footpath is easy: cross the mudflats, and, just before you reach the opposite bank, turn left and walk along the steep ascent. Continue until the edge of the woods swings to the right near the beach; this is where the trail enters the woods again. In case of high tide, you have two options: either wait for low tide, or cross the brook anyway. This is a wet affair; the eastern branches of Goose Creek may be only knee-deep, but the branch next to western bank is steep and can be in excess of 1 m (3 ft) deep. If you attempt a crossing, note that the creek generally gets deeper as it approaches the bay. However, walking upstream for any significant distance means bushwacking back on a steep hillside before continuing on the trail as described above in case of low tide.

As it enters the woods, the trail first leads inland, paralleling Goose Creek. Again, the trail is very steep and rugged and quite narrow in this area. After crossing two small creeks, the still narrow trail levels off and follows a ridge that allows some good views of the bay, including the Martin Head Peninsula ahead. The path ascends, then levels off, and follows a ravine to its right, which it crosses. The trail then begins to ascend, and, just before it reaches Brandy Brook, a 150 m/yd side trail departs to the right. The side trail follows the brook, crosses it, and reaches a pool below Tweedle Dee Tweedle Dum Falls.

Back on the main trail, the path ascends again. There are numerous switchbacks in the area, so mind the trail and its direction. There are some good views of Martin Head to enjoy. The path becomes fairly level in this area; it passes a small pond with dead trees on its right and crosses a grassy dirt road with a campground on its left at 11.3 km (7 mi). From here, the beach is accessible by turning to the left and then left again.

The trail crosses the grassy road straight ahead and leads away from the coast up through mature hardwoods, mostly beeches, paralleling the Martin Head dirt road. The trail crosses another small woods road, beyond which it starts a gradual but significant ascent. The forest becomes more open, and the trail swings to the left. At times, the Martin Head Road is visible to the left of the trail. The trail levels off, swings again to the left, and reaches the Martin Head access road at 12.8 km (8 mi). Note the red survey blazes in this area that follow the Footpath. The trail continues straight ahead on the other side of the road.

Section 4: MARTIN HEAD TO TELEGRAPH BROOK
The path leads away from the access road and descends immediately. In addition to the usual white blazes, there are many red blazes along the trail. The path turns right and crosses a gully. It descends and reaches Quiddy River at 13.4 km (8.3 mi), and the brook must be forded. The trail continues directly opposite, first through flood plains, and then it starts to ascend steeply through hardwoods, mostly birch trees. At 13.9 km (8.6 mi), the trail reaches an old woods road (the Old Martin Head Road). (The blue blazes to the right indicate a possible future trail.) The trail turns left onto that road, but swings off to the right soon after. It leads through fairly open mixed woods with many ferns.

You soon cross the woods road again. The forest is now dense with young growth, mostly beech trees. As the trail leads into softwoods, it starts to descend. A few small brooks must be crossed. Note the red surveying markings that still accompany the white-blazed trail. When you reach an old, fairly narrow woods road, the Footpath continues to the left towards the coast. As the trail moves into softwoods, you may catch glimpses of the coast to the left. At 17.3 km (10.8 mi), you reach Telegraph Brook. The trail continues on the opposite side of the creek a few steps farther towards the coast.

Section 5: TELEGRAPH BROOK TO WOLF BROOK. The trail climbs the steep hill in switchbacks. As it crosses a tiny creek, you again encounter red surveying blazes; do not follow them here. The trail descends to a small brook. A short distance beyond the crossing, a deep cut on the left allows a good view all the way down to the beach with its evolving seastacks. At 18.4 km (11.4 mi), note the yellow blazes of the Telegraph Brook exit trail that departs to the right. The Footpath descends a bit through mixed open forest with ferns. Walking is good in the area. As the trail continues close to the coast, it allows some views of Martin Head, which is now quite a distance away. The trail turns inland, then joins an old woods road and returns towards the coast. A hill opposite the steep ravine of Wolf Brook becomes visible. The very narrow trail descends in switchbacks towards Wolf Brook. The trail is very steep and slippery, especially towards the bottom of the descent. At 19.2 km (12.0 mi), the gravelly bed of meandering Wolf Brook is reached.

Section 6: WOLF BROOK TO DUSTAN BROOK. Once you reach Wolf Brook, turn right and follow the brook upstream on the east side. Pass by the remnants of two old logging dams. Directly beyond the second dam, ford the brook and turn into the woods directly towards a waterfall. Just before reaching it, the path turns off to the left. The narrow path ascends steeply though dense woods that alternate open areas. From now on, the trail continues through softwoods until its very end. The Footpath continues in a southwesterly direction, crossing a few wet spots and a logging dam. Then there are more wet spots, even some cotton grass, and a lot of moss. At 21.2 km (13.2 mi), a yellow-blazed exit trail departs to the right. The main trail descends to Rapidy Brook. Just before the trail reaches the brook, a small promontory on the left allows a view onto a waterfall downstream. Cross the brook straight ahead and climb. At 21.9 km (13.6 mi), the trail levels off and joins an old woods road, which it follows to the left. Turn off to the right a short distance later, and cross another woods road soon after.

The trail continues to climb at a gentle grade. As it peaks, there are some spectacular views onto a wide valley ahead. From here on, the Footpath descends, first steeply, then very steeply. As it levels off at 23.1 km (14.4 mi), it passes a campsite and reaches Dustan Brook. Turn right, walk some 30 m (100 ft) upstream, and cross the brook to its western bank. The Fundy Footpath terminates at another grassy campsite on the right at 23.2 km (14.4 mi). The high hills to the left are spectacular.

From this point on, the exit trail follows yellow (and sometimes green) blazes. Continue to the left into the woods, keep left at a fork, and, soon after, turn right onto a rocky woods road. The 2 m (6 ft) wide road switchbacks up for quite some time away from Dustan Brook. The trail levels off at 24 km (14.9 mi) and provides easy going from here on. There are some sizeable mud puddles that the trail bypasses, first to the right and then twice to the left of the woods road. After a while, the trail emerges out of the dark softwoods into a nice open area, and it reaches the road at 25.7 km (16 mi).

Trail Features: The Fundy Footpath provides access to one of the few remaining unspoiled areas in southern New Brunswick. Its main features are spectacular views of the Bay of Fundy, impressive tall cliffs, coastal forest alternating with beautiful hardwood ranges, and mountain brooks and waterfalls.

FUNDY NATIONAL PARK

View from the Coastal Trail. B. BERRY

FUNDY NATIONAL PARK

Fundy National Park, founded in 1950, is located on the Bay of Fundy, south-southwest of Moncton. The park is heavily forested, ranging from windswept coastal softwoods to beautiful hardwoods in its interior. The altitude ranges from sea level to about 365 m (1,200 ft); its surface measures 206 km^2 (80 mi^2) and there are some 100 km (60 mi) of hiking trails in the park. Some of the trails can be linked (see the map), thus forming a three- to five-day loop, the Fundy Circuit.

There are various types of accommodation in the park. In addition to a motel and chalets, there are four campgounds: Chignecto (212 sites), Headquarters (103 sites), Point Wolfe (181 sites), and Wolfe Lake (32 sites). These figures relate to the space available during the summer months; the capacity of the park campgrounds is substantially reduced during the other seasons. In addition, there are 14 wilderness campsites, which have to be reserved in advance. Some are equipped with picnic tables, firewood, and barbecue pits; all have pit toilets in the vicinity. Their locations and many details about all aspects of the park can be found in the park's newspaper, *Salt and Fir,* which is available at park headquarters as well as at the visitor centres located near the two park entrances. Additional information can be found in the book by Burzynski, which is listed in the Bibliography. Activities other than hiking include boating, fishing, bird-watching, tennis, lawn bowling and golfing; and golfers can enjoy the added pleasure spot-

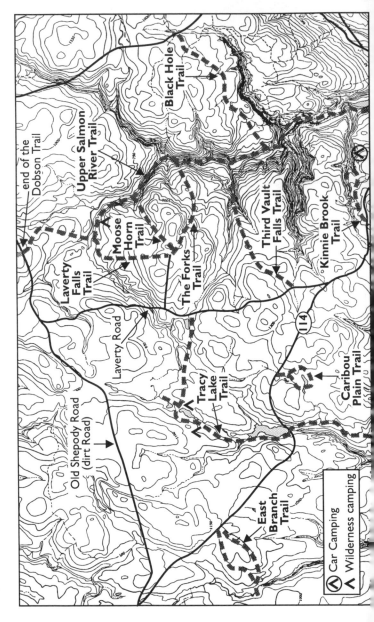

end of the
Dobson Trail

Upper Salmon
River Trail

Black Hole
Trail

Laverty
Falls
Trail

Moose
Horn
Trail

Third Vault
Falls Trail

Kinnie Brook
Trail

The Forks
Trail

Laverty Road

114

Old Shepody Road
(dirt Road)

Tracy
Lake
Trail

Caribou
Plain Trail

East
Branch
Trail

Ⓚ Car Camping

Ʌ Wilderness camping

Fundy National Park

ting deer on the 9-hole course. The nearby town of Alma offers accommodation, gas stations, restaurants, grocery stores and bike rentals.

Fundy National Park can be reached from Saint John and Fredericton by taking the Trans-Canada Highway (Highway 2) to 17 km (11 mi) east of Sussex. Turn right onto Highway 114 in a southeasterly direction and follow it about 25 km (16 miles) to the northwest entrance of the park. Access to all trails is described from here.

Two topographical maps cover Fundy National Park: 21 H/11 Waterford and 21 H/10 Alma. These maps, however, include only a few hiking trails. Hikers are considerably better served by the approximately 1:40,000 (1.5 inches to the mile) Fundy National Park Trail Guide, available at the Fundy visitor centres.

EAST BRANCH

Length: 5.6 km (3.5 mi)	**Hiking Time:** 1 hr 45 min
Type: loop	**Map:** Fundy National Park
Difficulty: easy	Trail Guide
Ascent: 70 m (200 ft)	**Trail Condition:** wide & dry

Access: From the northwest entrance of Fundy National Park at Wolfe Lake, follow Highway 114 for about 4 km (2.5 mi). The parking lot is located on the right side of the road. The trail starts there.

Trail Markings: The trail is groomed and obvious. There are a number of interpretive signs along the trail.

The Trail: The gravelly trail reaches a junction at 0.3 km (0.2 mi). Take the left path and follow the olive-and-yellow signs showing a hiker. The trail leads through nice, shady hardwood ridges. It passes "mystery mounds" (earthen mounds once thought to be Indian graves) and a swamp. At 2.8 km (1.7 mi), turn left at a T-junction and continue for some 300 m/yd to the remains of an old logging dam at the East Branch River. Even though there are no benches, this is an excellent place for a rest. Return to the junction and continue straight along an old, wide hauling road for about 2 km (1.2 mi). Turn left at the next junction and return to the parking lot.

Trail Features: The major attraction of the trail is a logging dam and yard at the East Branch of the Point Wolfe River. From here, logs were floated down the river to the sawmill at Point Wolfe.

BENNETT BROOK

Length: 15.8 km (9.8 mi) rtn
Type: linear
Difficulty: moderate, strenuous on both sides of the river
Ascent: 180 m (600 ft)

Map: Fundy National Park Trail Guide
Hiking Time: 5 hrs 30 min rtn
Trail Condition: dry, but two brooks must be forded

Access: From the park's northwest entrance at Wolfe Lake, follow Highway 114 for about 7 km (4.3 mi). Turn left at Bennett Lake into the parking area. The trailhead is located close to the dam.

Trail Markings: The first part of the trail is unmarked but cannot be missed. Beyond the end of the logging road, the descent to Point Wolfe River is marked by orange rectangles. The only confusing places are where Bennett Brook and Point Wolfe River must be forded.

The Trail: Cross the dam at Bennett Lake, crawl up the rather steep embankment and cross Highway 114. Here the trail first follows an old streambed, which is quite rocky. It soon swings left and the walking gets easier. The trail then leads through a forest where trilliums blossom in the spring. At 1.2 km (0.7 mi), the trail joins an old logging road. Turn right and follow this old road for about 3 km (2 mi). This part of the trail is easy as there are few ascents, and the road is lined with beech and birch trees as well as raspberry bushes. At about 4.2 km (2.6 mi), the road ends at a small turnaround.

At the far right corner of the turnaround, the path (now marked by orange metal rectangles) descends in steep switchbacks. The Point Wolfe River can sometimes be seen below. At 5.3 km (3.3 mi), the trail reaches the valley floor where it leaves the woods. Immediately to the right flows Bennett Brook, which joins the Point Wolfe River a little farther ahead. At this point it is necessary to ford Bennett Brook. Once across, turn left, follow the brook to its confluence with the Point Wolfe River, and follow that river upstream for about 50 m/yd. Here the Point Wolfe River must be forded. The trail continues almost straight ahead on the other side of the river. This continuation is clearly marked by a sign displaying a hiker.

For the next 1.6 km (1 mi), the trail ascends a steep and rocky hill. This part of the trail is strenuous. At 7.1 km (4.4 mi), the trail leaves the woods and ends at a wide grassy road. Turn right on that road, which in turn immediately swings to the left. (Turning left on the road leads you to Point Wolfe by way of the Marven Lake Trail.) Shortly after, a path departs to the left to Chambers Lake and wilderness campground #1. Continue straight on the main trail to campgrounds #2 and #3 at 7.9 km (4.9 mi). Beyond campground #3, the trail narrows and soon reaches the dark and boggy Marven Lake.

Trail Features: On the trail, the hiker can catch glimpses of the Point Wolfe River 150 m (500 ft) below. Small waterfalls and rapids in the Bennett Brook can be seen along the trail. At dawn or dusk, there is also a chance of seeing moose and beaver at Marven and Chambers lakes. Both lakes are shallow and dark, their colour resulting from acids that are released into the lakes from the bogs along their edges.

CARIBOU PLAIN TRAIL

Length: 3.4 km (2.1 mi)
Type: loop
Difficulty: easy
Ascent: 20 m (60 ft)

Hiking Time: 1 hr 15 min
Map: Fundy National Park Trail Guide
Trail Condition: dry, partly boardwalk

Access: From the northwest entrance of the park at Wolfe Lake, follow Highway 114 for about 9 km (5.6 mi). The trailhead is located at a parking lot on the right side of the road.

Trail Markings: None, but the trail is obvious.

The Trail: This interpretive nature trail passes a beaver dam and a bog before reaching a pond at 1.2 km (0.7 mi). After another 300 m/yd, a side trail departs to the left to an observation point with some benches at a small lake. This is a marvellous spot in the middle of a raised bog. At dawn and dusk, moose may be seen at the lake. Back on the main trail, the walk leads through a nice hardwood ridge with beech, maple and hobble bush. The trail returns to the parking lot on an old carriage road.

Trail Features: This very popular interpretive trail features a multitude of plants such as wood sorrel, cinnamon fern, cottongrass and various types of "bog bonsai" — plants that grow very slowly in the bog on account of its acidity. Red spruce and black (bog) spruce can also be seen along the trail. The major feature here is the raised bog with its sphagnum moss. Certain spots called "flarks" act like quicksand; a moose drowned at one flark in this bog a number of years ago.

TRACEY LAKE
(from Laverty Lake)

Length: 5.6 km (3.5 mi) rtn
Type: linear
Difficulty: easy to moderate
Ascent: 30 m (100 ft)

Hiking Time: 2 hrs rtn
Map: Fundy National Park Trail Guide
Trail Condition: wet spots, many rocks and roots

Access: From the northwest entrance of Fundy National Park at Wolfe Lake, follow Highway 114 for some 12 km (7.5 mi). Turn left onto Laverty Road and follow it for 4 km (2.5 mi). A parking lot is located next to Laverty Lake on the left; the trailhead is at the parking lot.

Trail Markings: None, but there are no forks and the trail is not difficult to follow.

The Trail: The trail follows the southern side of Laverty Lake for a while before continuing through the woods. At 1.1 km (0.7 mi), the trail crosses a creek, and there are some other wet spots that can be crossed on logs. The trail arrives at an excellent picnic site on Tracey Lake at 2.8 km (1.7 mi). There are two campsites in this area, both equipped with picnic tables, barbecue pits, a wood supply and a nearby pit toilet. From here, you can either return to Laverty Lake or explore nearby Bruin Lake on a short side trail before heading back. You can also continue the hike to Bennett Lake, which adds another 8.2 km (5.2 mi) (return) to the trip.

Trail Features: The trail connects two scenic lakes. There is a peaceful picnic site with a view of Tracey Lake at the end of the trail.

TRACEY LAKE
(from Bennett Lake)

Length: 8.2 km	**Hiking Time:** 3 hrs rtn
(5.2 mi) rtn	**Map:** Fundy National Park
Type: linear	Trail Guide
Difficulty: easy	**Trail Condition:** dry, some
Ascent: 30 m (100 ft)	rocks and roots

Access: From the northwest entrance of the park at Wolfe Lake, follow Highway 114 for about 7 km (4.4 mi). A large parking lot is located on the left side of the road next to Bennett Lake. Follow the paved path at the far right (northeast) end of the parking lot to the restrooms, continue to the beach, and turn left. The trailhead is located at the gate.

Trail Markings: None. As the trail is groomed and there are no forks or junctions, it is easy to follow.

The Trail: The trail proceeds with Bennett Lake on the right before swinging off to the left. It gently ascends, and at 1.1 km (0.7 mi) it reaches a very short side trail to the right that leads down to a small waterfall. The main trail crosses a creek at 1.3 km (0.8 mi). Beyond this crossing the trail gets narrower, and there are some rocks and roots, but the hiking is still pleasant hiking. At 3.3 km (2.1 mi) the trail reaches Tracey Lake, where it turns sharply to the left. This is also the location of a campsite.

The trail follows Tracey Lake through open forest, crosses a tiny creek by means of a boardwalk and reaches the northern edge of Tracey Lake. There are two campsites here as well as an excellent spot for a picnic. At this point, you can either return to Bennett Lake or take a short side trail to beautiful Bruin Lake along an old wagon road. (The road continues all the way to the Old Shepody Road but is not maintained beyond Bruin Lake.) Alternatively, you may continue the trail to Laverty Lake, another 5.6 km (3.4 mi) (return); see the Tracey Lake trail description.

Trail Features: This pleasant trail winds through open forest along two lakes. Moose are sometimes seen at peaceful Tracey Lake, where a beautiful picnic site is located.

COPPERMINE TRAIL

Length: 4.4 km (2.8 mi)　**Hiking Time:** 1 hr 45 min
Type: loop　**Map:** Fundy National Park
Difficulty: easy　Trail Guide
Ascent: 150 m (500 ft)　**Trail Condition:** dry

Access: From the northwest entrance of the park at
Wolfe Lake, follow Highway 114 for 19 km (12 mi) to
Park Headquarters. Turn right onto Point Wolfe Road
and follow it for 8 km (5 mi) to its end. The trailhead is
located at the far end of the parking lot.

Trail Markings: None, but the trail is well groomed and
cannot be missed.

The Trail: The level trail first leads through mixed forest, predominantly softwoods. At 0.6 km (0.4 mi), the
trail crosses a creek and immediately forks. Continue
straight/right. (The trail returns here on the left fork.)
The path now ascends gently but steadily through softwoods. At 2 km (1.2 mi), you will see tailings from an
old copper mine, which adventurous hikers may climb
up. From the top, you can see an old steam boiler
wedged in a very narrow but deep cut.

The main trail returns through softwoods. At 2.7 km
(1.7 mi), an unmarked side trail departs to the right,
leading to a lookout. The main trail continues for about
100 m/yd to a marked fork. A short trail to the right
leads to a nice picnic spot with two tables and a fine
view across the Bay of Fundy. The main trail has been
descending rather steeply, but its descent is more gentle
from this point on. The trail continues through softwoods and crosses a number of creeks, allowing some
glimpses of the bay to the right. It then continues
straight to the trailhead.

Trail Features: The main features of the trail are the remains of an old gold-and-copper mine which was operated from 1891 to 1910. Only the tailings and an old steam boiler remain today. Some pieces of quartz and tiny amounts of copper can be found in the tailings. The returning part of the trail features some fine views across the Bay of Fundy.

GOOSE RIVER TRAIL

Length: 15.8 km (9.8 mi) rtn
Type: linear
Difficulty: moderate
Ascent: 165 m (550 ft)

Hiking Time: 4 hrs 30 min rtn
Map: Fundy National Park Trail Guide
Trail Condition: dry

Access: From the northwest entrance of the park at Wolfe Lake, follow Highway 114 for 19 km (12 mi) to Park Headquarters. Turn right onto Point Wolfe Road and follow it for 8 km (5 mi) to its end. The trailhead is well marked and is located at the far end of the parking lot.

Trail Markings: The trail is unmarked, but it follows an old cartroad and cannot be missed.

The Trail: Not far from the trailhead, the trail joins a wide, old cart road which provided access to the tiny settlement of Goose River in the last century. The trail soon turns left, and for the next 1 km (0.6 mi) it ascends steadily. The well-marked junction with the Marven Lake and Rattail trails is 1 km (0.6 mi) from the trailhead. Continue straight and cross Mile Brook at 3.7 km (2.3 mi). Some overgrown clearings to both sides of the trail indicate the sites of old settlements. At 7.9 km (4.9

mi), the trail reaches campsite #4, located on a high bluff overlooking the rocky coastline. This is a spectacular view that should not be missed.

The trail now becomes narrow and leads down to the beach. It passes campsite #5, then swings sharply to the right and descends steeply. At the beach, there are two farther campsites near the Bay of Fundy and the mouth of the meandering Goose River. It is definitely worthwhile to explore the beach and Goose River (which shelters a small salt marsh) before heading back.

Trail Features: A pleasant hike past the overgrown old settlement of Goose River; its schoolyard, rock foundations, and gooseberry bushes are silent witnesses of a bygone era. There are some fine views of the rocky coastline of the Bay of Fundy. Beachcombing and watching the change of the giant tides are favourite activities.

MARVEN LAKE TRAIL

Length: 16 km (10 mi) rtn
Type: linear
Difficulty: easy to moderate
Ascent: 210 m (700 ft)

Hiking Time: 4 hrs 30 min rtn
Map: Fundy National Park Trail Guide
Trail Condition: dry, wide old road

Access: From the northwest entrance of the park at Wolfe Lake, follow Highway 114 for 19 km (12 mi) to Park Headquarters. Turn right onto Point Wolfe Road and follow it for 8 km (5 mi) to its end. The trailhead is located at the far end of the parking lot.

Trail Markings: None, but as the trail follows a wide, old wagon road, it cannot be missed.

The Trail: The first part of the Marven Lake Trail duplicates the Goose River Trail. From the trailhead, a path leads through a small forest and very soon reaches an old grassy wagon road, which turns left and rises slowly. At 1 km (0.6 mi), keep right at a fork. The trail here follows another wide and mostly level road with a few gentle ascents. At 3.4 km (2.1 mi), the Foster Brook Trail departs to the right. Continue straight on the wide road. It is lined with young growth and provides for an uneventful and easy hike. Hikers can stroll side by side. At one point you must cross a wet spot, caused by a poorly drained brook. At 7.2 km (4.5 mi), Bennett Brook Trail departs to the right and the main road makes a sharp left turn. Just beyond the turn, a short side trail to the left leads down to quiet Chambers Lake, where there is a campsite. The main trail continues for a short distance, passes two wilderness campsites, and ends at boggy Marven Lake.

Trail Features: The trail gives access to two shallow wilderness lakes. Chambers and Marven lakes are dark with acids from their boggy edges. They provide a home for brook trout, bullfrogs, moose and beaver.

SHIPHAVEN TRAIL

Length: 1 km (0.6 mi) rtn **Hiking Time:** 45 min rtn
Type: linear **Map:** Fundy National Park
Difficulty: easy Trail Guide
Ascent: 45 m (150 ft) **Trail Condition:** partly
boardwalk

Access: From the northwest entrance of the park at Wolfe Lake, follow Highway 114 for 19 km (12 mi) to Park Headquarters. Turn right onto Point Wolfe Road and follow it for 8 km (5 mi) to its end at a parking lot with about 35 parking spaces. The trailhead is located to the right of the toilets.

Trail Markings: None, but the short trail cannot be missed.

The Trail: This well-groomed, partly boardwalk trail leads through a stand of tall softwoods. It then starts to descend, keeping the mouth of the Point Wolfe River to its right. There are some fine views of the inlet and the surrounding cliffs. The trail terminates at the western end of a bridge. The covered bridge across the Point Wolfe River was accidentally destroyed by workers in late December 1990. It has been replaced by a new covered bridge. From here you can see remnants of an old dam, part of an earlier sawmill operation.

Trail Features: This trail is worthwhile for the interesting views across the mouth of the Point Wolfe River and the bay as well as some remains from the old sawmill days. The Shiphaven Trail was built in 1989/90.

FOSTER BROOK TRAIL

Length: 4.8 km (3 mi) one way [to Point Wolfe River 3.2 Km (2 mi) rtn]
Type: linear
Difficulty: moderate
Ascent: 210 m (700 ft)

Hiking Time: 1 hr 30 min one way [to Point Wolfe River 1hr 15 min rtn]
Map: Fundy National Park Trail Guide
Trail Condition: dry, one ford

Access: From the northwest entrance of the park at Wolfe Lake, follow Highway 114 for 19 km (12 mi) to Park Headquarters. Turn right onto Point Wolfe Road and follow it for 5.8 km (3.6 mi), then turn right again onto a gravel road. Turn right at a fork and park at some grassy spot. There is room for about eight vehicles. The trailhead is located at the far left of the parking lot.

Trail Markings: None, but the trail is clearly defined.

The Trail: The trail ascends rather steeply for a short distance, then it continues up gentler grades through softwoods. At 1.6 km (1 mi), the trail slopes steeply downwards for some 300 m/yd until it reaches a junction. A short but definitely worthwhile spur gives access to Point Wolfe River. (Weary hikers may turn around here and still claim to have hiked to Point Wolfe River!)

The main trail turns sharply to the right. The trail crosses Foster Brook on a wooden bridge and continues to follow Point Wolfe River for 1.3 km (0.8 mi) to a junction at the Rattail wilderness campground. This part of the trail is level and hiking is easy. A short spur to the left leads down to the campsites and the river. The main trail continues straight for a short distance before turning sharply to the left. (The trail that continues straight is the old Rattail Trail, which is officially closed and no longer maintained by the park.) The trail descends to the Point Wolfe River.

Ford the cobblestone riverbed and reach the continuation of the trail directly across at 3.4 km (2.1 mi). From here, the trail ascends steeply through old-growth red spruce forest before its ascent becomes more gentle. It reaches the Marven Lake Trail at 4.8 km (3 mi).

Trail Features: The red maples and yellow birches along the river are quite spectacular, especially in the fall. The Point Wolfe River is once again the home to Atlantic salmon through a dam alteration and re-stocking program. The mature red spruce forest is also worth noting.

SQUAWS CAP LOOP

Length: 4.9 km (3 mi)
Type: loop
Difficulty: easy to moderate
Ascent: 100 m (350 ft)

Hiking Time: 1 hr 30 min
Map: Fundy National Park Trail Guide
Trail Condition: a few wet spots

Access: From the northwest park entrance at Wolfe Lake, follow Highway 114 for 19 km (12 mi) to the junction at Park Headquarters. Turn right onto Point Wolfe Road and follow it for about 5.8 km (3.6 mi), then turn left onto Herring Cove Road. Follow it for 1.6 km (1 mi), then turn right onto a gravel road. This road first turns left, goes behind a building, and then turns right again. There are about 10 parking places at the trailhead.

Trail Markings: None, but the trail is well defined and cannot be missed.

The Trail: This grassy trail follows an old wagon road through fields and softwoods. The first part of the trail is known as is the Matthews Head Trail. At 0.8 km (0.5 mi), it reaches Matthews Head field and starts descending. The trail passes by the remains of an old homestead settled by Thomas Matthews in the early 1800s. At a junction, continue straight/left for another 200 m/yd, where you reach Matthews Head. This outcrop offers a beautiful view of the Bay of Fundy. You can see the town of Alma from here as well as a little bay with a sandy beach to the left of Matthews Head. Return to the junction, turn left, and follow the narrower path along the coast to Squaws Cap Overlook with its bench. Just beyond the lookout, the trail swings inland and reaches a junction at 3.9 km (2.4 mi). Complete the loop by turning right. The trail ascends through woods until it reaches a large field. The well-defined trail turns right, follows the edge of the woods, and then crosses the field where there are many wildflowers and raspberries in season. From here, the trail returns to the parking lot.

Trail Features: The trail features the foundations of the old Matthews homestead as well as spectacular views across the Bay of Fundy, including Squaws Cap, a sea-stack.

DEVILS HALF ACRE

Length: 1.1 km (0.7 mi)
Type: loop
Difficulty: easy
Ascent: 60 m (200 ft)

Hiking Time: 30 min
Map: Fundy National Park Trail Guide
Trail Condition: dry, partly boardwalk

Access: From the northwest entrance of the park at Wolfe Lake, follow Highway 114 for 19 km (12 mi) to Park Headquarters. Turn right onto Point Wolfe Road and follow it for 1.2 km (0.7 mi). Turn left and continue on that road for another 1.2 km (0.7 mi), where a parking lot is located on the left side of the road. The lot accommodates about eight vehicles.

Trail Markings: None, but the trail is very well groomed and is impossible to miss.

Trail Features: The main feature of this trail is its geology. The deep cuts, cracks, and split rocks are formed as rainwater seeps through the sandstone into a layer of shale. In freezing temperatures, the water expands and the cracks get wider. Rock movements of up to 20 cm (8 inches) annually have been recorded. Gaping holes, split rocks, fallen and uprooted trees make the area look like the devil's work.

DICKSON FALLS

Length: 1 km (0.6 mi)   **Hiking Time:** 30 min
Type: loop   **Map:** Fundy National Park
Difficulty: easy   Trail Guide
Ascent: negligible   **Trail Condition:** dry

Access: From the northwest entrance of the park at Wolfe Lake, follow Highway 114 for 19 km (12 mi) to Park Headquarters. Turn right onto Point Wolfe Road and follow it for 2 km (1.2 mi). There is a large parking lot here with a fine lookout at its end. The trailhead is located opposite the toilets.

Trail Markings: None. This trail is very well groomed and is easy to follow.

The Trail: The trail descends gently through open, mixed forest. At a fork, a very short side trail departs straight ahead. At its end, a platform allows an excellent view of the Dickson Falls. The main trail turns right, follows a brook, then crosses it twice on wooden bridges before returning to the parking lot.

Trail Features: The major attractions of this very popular trail are the Dickson Falls and the healthy forest, which has successfully bounced back after suffering budworm damage.

SHADED MAPLES TRAIL

Length: 0.5 km (0.3 mi) **Hiking Time:** 15 min
Type: loop **Map:** Fundy National Park
Difficulty: easy Trail Guide
Ascent: negligible **Trail Condition:** dry

Access: From the northwest entrance of the park at Wolfe Lake, follow Highway 114 for 19 km (12 mi) to Park Headquarters. Turn right onto Point Wolfe Road and follow it for 3.2 km (2 mi). Turn right onto Hastings Road (a gravel road), and immediately turn right again onto Maple Grove Road. Continue on this road for 1 km (0.6 mi). On the left side of the road there is space for about eight to ten vehicles. The trailhead is on the right side of the road.

Trail Markings: None, but this well-groomed trail is obvious and cannot be missed.

Trail Features: This trail is especially pretty in the fall when the colours change. More than 10 different ferns carpet the forest floor. Note the white quartz rocks along the trail.

COASTAL TRAIL

Length: 20.2 km (12.6 mi) rtn
Type: linear
Difficulty: moderate
Ascent: 150 m (500 ft)

Hiking Time: 8 hrs rtn
Map: Fundy National Park Trail Guide
Trail Condition: Some wet spots

Access: From the northwest park entrance at Wolfe Lake, follow Highway 114 for 19 km (12 mi) to the junction at Park Headquarters. Turn right onto Point Wolfe Road and follow it for 600 m/yd. The trailhead is located on the right just beyond an old stone bridge. Numerous parking spaces are available next to the rocky beach at the end of the short road that turns off to the left behind the stone bridge.

Trail Markings: Some weathered orange metal blazes are found along the trail, but its course is obvious.

The Trail: The trail ascends steeply for a short distance before it crosses the two-lane paved road to Devils Half Acre. The trail continues to climb for quite some time, but more gently now. The forest here is mixed, but soft-woods dominate, and there are some good views overlooking the bay. The trail then descends rather steeply to a T-junction at 2.8 km (1.7 mi). At this point, the Whitetail Trail turns right whereas the Coastal Trail continues to the left, leading to the Herring Cove parking lot. A nice seaward view with some interpretive displays and a telescope await the visitor here. From the picnic site with a pit toilet, a short path leads down to the beach at Herring Cove.

The trail continues straight across the parking lot and picnic site to the right of a shelter. It dips down to a creek and crosses it. Keep right at a fork; the left fork leads back to Herring Cove. Just beyond a lookout across the bay, keep right again. The trail starts ascending through very pretty hardwoods. Beyond a plateau, the trail descends through mixed woods to Matthews Head. There is a good view across the bay at this point with a small cove immediately to the left and the town of Alma straight ahead in the distance. The trail continues to the right and turns left at a junction.

The trail crosses two short boardwalks before the bay becomes visible again. From this point on, the trail is quite level, with the bay visible from time to time. The trail traverses a meadow in the woods, where there may be wet spots. Beyond the meadow, the trail ascends to an excellent lookout over the bay. From here you can see the Squaw's Cap, a rock in the bay in the shape of a flower pot. The trail then descends, crosses a small brook, and continues through mixed forest. It then swings into the woods away from the bay. At 9.5 km (5.9 mi), the trail starts sloping down, swings in a westerly direction, and then the descent gets steep. The trail terminates at the Point Wolfe Road across from a parking lot at the Point Wolfe River.

Trail Features: The main features of this trail are the frequent lookouts across the Bay of Fundy. The remains of the Thomas Matthews farm, built in 1865, can be seen along the trail. Thomas Matthews's father John was among the first settlers to arrive in the area, and he obtained land grants for the best farmland in what is now Fundy National Park.

WHITETAIL TRAIL

Length: 12.2 km (7.6 mi)
Type: loop
Difficulty: moderate to strenuous
Ascent: 240 m (800 ft)

Map: Fundy National Park Trail Guide
Hiking Time: 4 hrs 30 min
Trail Condition: dry

Access: From the northwest park entrance at Wolfe Lake, follow Highway 114 for 16 km (10 mi) to the Chignecto Campground. Turn left and immediately right again to the parking lot. The trailhead is located on the far right of the parking lot.

Trail Markings: Some older 2" x 4" red and orange metal blazes are found along the way, but even without them the trail is easy to find.

The Trail: From the trailhead at the Chignecto parking lot, a well-groomed, gravelly trail skirts the campground. It crosses the main road (Highway 114) near a blind hill, and soon passes by the remains of an old homestead. The trail continues through mixed forest and crosses a brook underneath some power lines. At 1.2 km (0.7 mi), it reaches a junction. Take the left path and continue on the rather rocky trail. Soon two creeks are crossed, then the trail swings to the right, keeping the brook to its right in a valley below. The trail descends and crosses two brooks. Just beyond the second crossing there is a maze of little trails. Keep to the left with the golf course to the right. The trail appears to end at the orchard of an old homestead with the golf course still to the right. Continue along the edge of the golf course, walk over the ridge on the left, and then cross the Point Wolfe Road and walk across a stone bridge.

The path continues to the right, just beyond the bridge, at 4.3 km (2.7 mi). This part of the Whitetail Trail coincides with the Coastal Trail (see the trail description on page 151.) The trail ascends steeply for a short distance and then crosses the two-lane, paved road to Devils Half Acre. It continues to rise for quite some time, but more gently now. The forest here consists predominantly of softwoods, and there are some good view across the bay. The trail then descends rather steeply to a T-junction at 7.1 km (4.4 mi). Here the Whitetail Trail continues to the right, while the Coastal Trail turns to the left where a 250 m/yd side trail leads to the Herring Cove parking lot. A nice seaward lookout with some interpretive displays and a telescope await the visitor here. From the picnic site (with a pit toilet), a short trail leads down to the beach.

Back at the junction, the trail ascends steeply for a while before levelling off. Just beyond some fine views, the trail drops very steeply into the Dickson Brook valley. Note the beaver pond whose dam is located next to the trail. Not far beyond the dam, the trail crosses the Point Wolfe Road at 8.8 km (5.5 mi). After a short, moderate incline the trail is reasonably flat, with a few ups and downs, and it crosses a number of creeks. Note some white quartz rocks along the way. This is an area of very pretty hardwoods. At one point the trail is obscured; watch for the orange and red blazes. The trail reaches a junction at 11 km (6.9 mi). From here the trail is familiar to you; continue straight ahead and return to the Chignecto parking lot.

Trail Features: There is a good chance of seeing whitetail deer, especially near the golf course. Along the stretch where the Whitetail and Coastal trails coincide, there are some fine views across the Bay of Fundy. A beaver dam and pond can also be seen in the Dickson Brook valley.

UPPER SALMON RIVER TRAIL

Length: 15.8 km
(10 mi) one way
Type: linear
Ascent: 180 m (600 ft)
Difficulty: moderate to
difficult

Map: Fundy National Park
Trail Guide
Hiking Time: 7 hrs one way
Trail Condition: dry,
several fords, rock
scrambling between The
Forks and Moosehorn

Summary:
Section 1: 4.7 km (2.9 mi), 2 hrs, 1 ford
Section 2: 4.1 km (2.6 mi), 1 hr 30 min, 2 fords
Section 3: 1.8 km (1.1 mi), 1 hr 30 min, 2 fords
Section 4: 2.6 km (1.6 mi), 1 hr
Section 5: 2.6 km (1.6 mi), 1 hr, 1 ford

Access: From the northwest entrance of the park at
Wolfe Lake, follow Highway 114 for 19 km (12 mi) to
the park headquarters. There is a parking lot here. The
trailhead is located a short distance away, opposite the
road to the campground.

Note: Hikers can combine this trail with the Dobson
Trail or hike only parts of it if they do not intend to
camp. The following individual linear sections can be
combined with other trails, such as the Black Hole, The
Forks, Moosehorn, and Laverty Falls trails. You can
leave a second vehicle at the trailheads of the chosen
hiking trail (see map.)

Trail Markings: The trail is unmarked with the exception of the last section, from Laverty Falls to the
Shepody Road, which is marked by faded 2" x 4" white
metal blazes. Most of the trail is fairly obvious, but the
trail is obscured in some places.

The Trail:

Section 1: HEADQUARTERS TO BLACK HOLE. The well-groomed trail leads through mixed forest across some boardwalk sections. At one point, another trail from the campground joins from the right. The trail starts to ascend and reaches a cabin. Cross the gravelly area and little Kinnie Brook and follow the Upper Salmon River, keeping it to the right. At 2.3 km (1.4 mi), the trail makes a sharp turn to the right; you must ford the river. A steel cable has been installed to help you across. The path then follows the east bank of the Upper Salmon River. The trail soon narrows and ascends, and it gets rocky and rooty. Cross Lake Brook via some rocks, and soon you reach a ranger cabin (Warden Station) at Black Hole. Atlantic salmon rest in the Black Hole pool in the fall before swimming upstream to spawn. In summer, this spot serves as a refreshing pool for humans.

Section 2: BLACK HOLE TO FORKS. The trail continues on the east side of the river, past the cabin and a pit toilet, and crosses several small creekbeds (usually dry). Note the Upper Vault Brook across the river. Continue through mixed forest on the stony but mostly level trail. At 8.8 km (5.5 mi), you reach the confluence of the Broad and Forty-Five rivers. Ford the Forty-Five River just above the confluence and continue on the other side.

Section 3: THE FORKS TO MOOSEHORN. Soon, a cable across the Broad River becomes visible to the left; it aids the ford to the Forks Trail. To continue along the Upper Salmon River Trail, do not ford here, but stay on the east side of the Broad River upstream while you hike along its narrow and rocky streambed. A sign indicates the start of a 1.8-km (1.1 mi) stretch that is difficult and rather strenuous, as it requires some scrambling hopping from rock to rock. Occasional iron rungs help with climbing across huge boulders. At other points along this section, the path ascends into the woods and dips down again to the rocky riverbed. Pass the scenic Broad River Falls and ford the Broad River as indicated by a sign on the west side of the river. Continue on the trail along the river. The Moosehorn Trail departs to the left at 10.6 km (6.6 mi).

Section 4: MOOSEHORN TO LAVERTY FALLS. This trail passes some interesting rounded boulders, the remnants of an old logging dam, and then alternates between stretches of alder-lined riverbank and gravelly streamsides. The trail passes the remains of another dam and soon continues along a now very tame river. In a gravelly area at the confluence of the Broad River and Haley Brook, the trail turns left (westward) and follows Haley Brook.

Section 5: LAVERTY FALLS TO SHEPODY ROAD. At 13.2 km (8.2 mi), the trail reaches a sign saying "To Shepody Road". The Laverty Falls Trail continues straight, but to stay on the Upper Salmon River Trail, turn right at this sign and ford Haley Brook. The trail then continues straight into the woods. It is a very narrow path now, marked by white blazes. The trail leads through softwoods, raspberry bushes and blueberry patches. It first follows Haley Brook before turning off to the right. The trail ends at Shepody Road directly opposite a logging road, which is also one end of the Dobson Trail.

Trail Features: The major feature of this trail is the Upper Salmon River with its steep valley walls, gorges, waterfalls, salmon pools and alder-lined floodplains. Remnants of logging dams can be seen along the Broad River. Limited tenting is permitted along the river by registering at the park headquarters.

BLACK HOLE TRAIL

Length: 11 km (6.8 mi) rtn
Type: linear
Difficulty: easy to moderate
Ascent: 210 m (700 ft)

Hiking Time: 3 hrs 30 min rtn
Map: Fundy National Park Trail Guide
Trail Condition: dry, wide cart road

Access: From the northwest park entrance at Wolfe Lake, follow Highway 114 to the park exit at Alma. Continue on Highway 114 for 3.4 km (2.1 mi) and then turn left onto Forty-Five Road. Follow this rough gravel road for 2 km (1.2 mi) to a fork. Keep left. The road crosses a bridge, then turns left into a parking lot.

Trail Markings: None. This is an old cart road with no side trails departing from it, so the trail is easy to follow.

The Trail: The trail first leads through mixed forest with some raspberry bushes along the way. At 1.8 km (1.1 mi), it crosses a small creek. The trail then passes through a beautiful stand of young hardwoods, mostly maple and beech. It crosses another creek on some rocks at 2.8 km (1.7 mi). To this point the trail has been flat. Beyond the creek, it gently slopes downward. At 4.8 km (3 mi), the trail drops sharply until it reaches a T-junction with the Upper Salmon River Trail. There is a pit toilet. Turn left and soon you reach a ranger's log cabin and the Upper Salmon River.

Trail Features: The main feature of the trail is the Black Hole in the Upper Salmon River. In late summer and fall, Atlantic salmon stay here for a while before they move upstream to spawn. This is a very pleasant hike to a river that is scenically located in a valley.

THE FORKS TRAIL

Length: 6.8 km (4.2 mi) rtn
Type: linear
Difficulty: moderate to strenuous
Ascent: 275 m (900 ft)

Map: Fundy National Park Trail Guide
Hiking Time: 3 hrs 30 min rtn
Trail Condition: dry

Access: From the northwest entrance of the park at Wolfe Lake, follow Highway 114 for 12 km (7.5 mi), then turn left onto Laverty Road. After 5 km (3.1 mi) on this gravel road, turn right at a junction. Follow this road for 1.6 km (1 mi) to a turnaround. The parking lot here accommodates about 12 vehicles. There is also a log cabin and a pit toilet. The trailheads of the Moosehorn and The Forks trails are straight ahead; the Laverty Falls Trail begins on the left.

Trail Markings: Orange and red metal 2" x 4" blazes on trees.

The Trail: The trail descends to a fork at 0.2 km (0.1 mi) and continues straight ahead (the left fork leads down the Moosehorn Trail). The Forks Trail first ascends gradually but soon descends rather steeply. On its way down it passes a sometime pond on its left. At 2.3 km (1.4 mi), a little creek becomes visible to the right and the trail reaches a fork. Stay right and cross the creek. At about 3 km (1.9 mi), there is a nice view to the right of the opposite slope. The trail crosses the small creek again and soon reaches its end at the Broad River. The river has remarkably deep pools, which provide a rest stop for spawning salmon. From here, you may either return the way your came or ford the Broad River twice and return on the Moosehorn or Laverty Falls trails (see the trail descriptions on page 160 and page 161).

Trail Features: The main feature is the narrow gorge at the end of the trail. The Broad River has some deep holes here. In the fall, Atlantic salmon rest here when they come up to spawn; they can be observed in these holes. Fly fishing for salmon is allowed, provided you have a National Park fishing permit.

MOOSEHORN TRAIL

Length: 4.4 km (2.8 mi) rtn
Type: linear
Difficulty: moderate
Ascent: 215 m (700 ft)

Hiking Time: 2 hrs 30 min rtn
Map: Fundy National Park Trail Guide
Trail Condition: dry

Access: From the northwest entrance of the park at Wolfe Lake, follow Highway 114 for 12 km (7.5 mi), then turn left onto Laverty Road. After 5 km (3.1 mi) on this gravel road, turn right at a junction. Follow this road for 1.6 km (1 mi) to a turnaround. The parking lot here accommodates about 12 vehicles. There is also a log cabin and a pit toilet. The trailheads of the Moosehorn and The Forks trails are straight ahead; Laverty Falls Trail begins on the left.

Trail Markings: None, but the trail is clearly defined and easy to follow.

The Trail: The Moosehorn Trail, named after a logger's portage, descends right away to a fork at 0.2 km (0.1 mi). Turn left. (The Forks Trail continues straight ahead.) The path leads through magnificent mixed forest and crosses a little brook, keeping the brook to its left and at a distance. At 1.8 km (1.1 mi), the gentle grade downwards steepens considerably. At a fork, a short side trail departs to the left to the foot of a waterfall. The main trail continues straight and reaches a fork at the Broad River. This is the end of the Moosehorn Trail.

Rather than turning back, you can turn left, follow the river for 2.6 km (1.6 mi) to Laverty Falls, and return to the parking lot by the 2.5 km (1.6 mi) long Laverty Falls Trail. Another more difficult route is to turn right and follow the river to the end of The Forks Trail. This requires fording the Upper Salmon River twice. For a description, see the appropriate section of the Upper Salmon River Trail. If you take this option, you must return on The Forks Trail, which is rather steep.

Trail Features: A trail through nice mixed forest, a waterfall, and access to the midsection of the Broad River.

LAVERTY FALLS TRAIL

Length: 5 km (3.2 mi) rtn **Hiking Time:** 2 hrs 15 min
Type: linear   rtn
Difficulty: easy to   **Map:** Fundy National Park
moderate   Trail Guide
Ascent: 185 m (600 ft)   **Trail Condition:** dry

Access: From the northwest entrance of the park at Wolfe Lake, follow Highway 114 for 12 km (7.5 mi), then turn left onto Laverty Road. After 5 km (3.1 mi) on this gravel road, turn right at a junction. Follow this road for 1.6 km (1 mi) to a turnaround. The parking lot here accommodates about 12 vehicles. There is also a log cabin and a pit toilet. The trailheads of the Moosehorn and The Forks trails are straight ahead; the Laverty Falls Trail begins on the left.

Trail Markings: Some older 2" x 4" orange metal blazes are found along the trail, but it is obvious and easy to follow.

The Trail: The trail descends gently but steadily through magnificent hardwoods, mostly maple. At 2.3 km (1.4 mi), the trail turns sharply to the right. A small lookout straight ahead overlooks the head of the Laverty Falls. A short distance farther along, a side trail departs to the left. It leads to the foot of the falls, a nice place for a rest. The main trail continues to a fork at the confluence of the Haley and Laverty brooks. Here you may turn left to the Old Shepody Road (see the description of the Upper Salmon River Trail) or right to the Moosehorn Trail or The Forks Trail, or even all the way down the Upper Salmon River towards the park headquarters.

Trail Features: The main features of the trail are the beautiful hardwoods it leads through, as well as the many wildflowers found here, especially in spring. Also remarkable are the Laverty Falls and the unspoiled brooks at the end of the trail.

KINNIE BROOK TRAIL

Length: 2.8 km (1.8 mi) rtn

Type: linear

Difficulty: easy

Ascent: 130 m (450 ft)

Hiking Time: 1 hr 15 min rtn

Map: Fundy National Park Trail Guide

Trail Condition: dry

Access: Entering the park from the northwest entrance at Wolfe Lake, follow Highway 114 for about 15 km (9.5 mi). The trailhead is on the left side of the road next to a picnic area.

Trail Markings: The trail is marked by yellow metal triangular blazes.

The Trail: This interpretive trail leads through a moderately shady forest. At 0.8 km (0.5 mi), a short trail to a campground departs to the right. The main trail continues straight and level for some time before descending. Notice the steep gorge on the left. At one point, wooden stairs lead down and up again before the trail finally descends a long flight of stairs to Kinnie Brook at the valley floor. On its downward path, the trail passes an imposing rock on the right. The trail ends at a wooden platform overlooking the brook, where an interpretive sign explains some features of the brook. Here hikers can explore some small waterfalls in the vicinity of the trail's end.

Trail Features: The stream at the bottom of the steep-walled gorge disappears at times. Its banks are densely overgrown, and red-osier dogwood, ferns and cow parsnip grow on the floodplain.

THIRD VAULT FALLS TRAIL

Length: 7.4 km (4.6 mi) rtn
Type: linear
Difficulty: easy to moderate
Ascent: 150 m (500 ft)

Hiking Time: 2 hrs 30 min rtn
Map: Fundy National Park Trail Guide
Trail Condition: dry

Access: Entering Fundy National Park from the northwest at Wolfe Lake, follow Highway 114 for about 12 km (7.5 mi). Turn left onto Laverty Road (a dirt road in good condition) and follow it for 1 km (0.6 mi). The trailhead is located at the far end of the parking lot on the right.

Trail Markings: None, but the trail is obvious and easy to follow.

The Trail: For the first part, the surface of the trail is gravel. Beyond that, it becomes a regular forest trail with some rocky spots. For its entire length, the trail lies in semi-shade, which makes hiking pleasant in the summer. Except for the last 0.8 km (0.5 mi), the trail is flat. Towards the end it descends steeply, in part on wooden stairs. Once the Upper Vault Brook is reached, the trail swings to the left. In order to see the falls, you must cross a small brook. The falls can be seen at the trail-end on the left, where the impressive waterfall plunges into a round pool.

Trail Features: The main attraction of this trail is the waterfall. At 16 m (53 ft), these are the highest falls in the park.

EASTERN SHORES

New Horton Marsh. H.A. EISELT

EASTERN SHORES

New Brunswick's Eastern shores are composed of a number of distinct areas, ranging from alluvial marshes along the southeastern shores to sandbars along the Northumberland Strait and the Bay of Chaleur.

The biggest city of this region is Moncton, New Brunswick's second largest city. It was named in honour of Colonel Robert Monckton, commander of the British forces that in 1755 captured Fort Beauséjour, which was subsequently called Fort Cumberland. Later, the French name was revived and is still in use today. Moncton is home of New Brunswick's first multi-day hiking trail, the Dobson Trail, which runs from Moncton-Riverview to Fundy National Park.

The university town of Sackville in southeastern New Brunswick is located near the centre of a marshland that has been reclaimed from the sea. In the early days, the Acadians accomplished that task by building so-called aboiteaux, systems of dikes and dams. Near Sackville, formerly known as Tantramar, are the Tantramar Marshes. The name is derived from the French word "tintamarre," which means din or noise and refers to the sound made by large flocks of geese when taking flight. Not surprisingly, bird hunting is still very popular in the area.

Shediac, the "Lobster Capital of the World," is located on the Eastern shores at the Northumberland Strait. Here, you find the warmest salt water beaches north of Virginia. Along the shores is the small town of

Bouctouche, birthplace of the late K.C. Irving, one of the richest men in the world, and Antonine Maillet, renowned Acadian author. At the northern end of the Northumberland Strait is Kouchibouguac National Park, a nature lover's paradise. Sandy beaches and lagoons, saltmarshes and bogs are characteristic for the area.

The city of Miramichi meets the ocean, where international ships take on wood products and where the Irish and Scots celebrate their heritage with fiddles and backpipes each summer. Miramichi was the home of three famous people: newspaper magnate and benefactor Lord Beaverbrook (Sir Max Aitken), shipping magnate Joseph Cunard and R.B. Bennett, the only prime minister born in New Brunswick.

The coastal forest bog with its distinguishing black spruce and stunted larches is characteristic for the northern tip of the Acadian Peninsula. Here, peat moss operations and fisheries are the mainstays of the economy. Near Caraquet is the Acadian Historical Village, which depicts the life of early settlers in the 18th century. The northern communities of Caraquet, Bathurst, and Dalhousie are strung along miles of sandy beaches of the Bay of Chaleur. It was off this coast that the last naval battle for the possession of Canada between the British and the French took place in 1760.

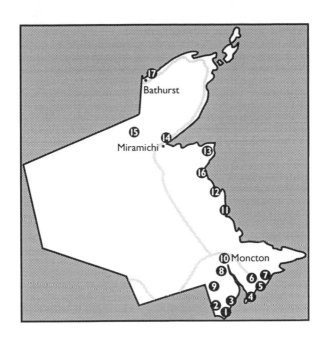

Eastern Shores

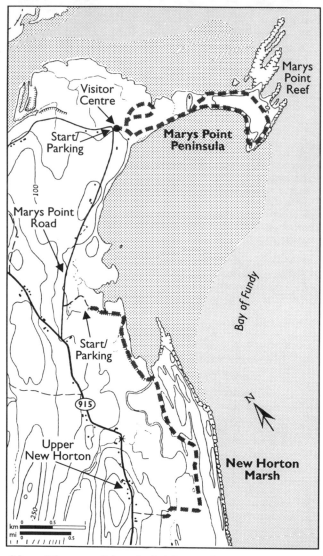

Visitor Centre

Start/ Parking

Marys Point Road

Start/ Parking

Marys Point Reef

Marys Point Peninsula

Bay of Fundy

915

Upper New Horton

New Horton Marsh

N

km
mi

New Horton Marsh & Marys Point Peninsula

NEW HORTON MARSH

Length: 9 km (5.6 mi) rtn
Type: linear
Difficulty: easy
Ascent: negligible

Hiking Time: 2 hrs 30 min rtn
Map: 21 H/10 Alma
Trail Condition: some wet spots

Access: From Moncton, take Highway 114 south to Riverside-Albert. Turn left onto Highway 915 and follow it for 5.4 km (3.4 mi). Turn left onto Marys Point Road. After 500 m/yd, turn right onto another gravel road and follow it for 500 m/yd. There is parking space for about four to six vehicles.

Alternatively, take Highway 915 east out of Alma, near Fundy National Park, and follow the road for about 30 km (19 mi) before turning right onto Marys Point Road.

Trail Markings: None. As there are no forks or junctions, the trail cannot be missed.

The Trail: The trail follows the top of a dike in a southeasterly direction and overlooks the bay inlet and marshland. At 0.5 km (0.3 mi), the path turns sharply to the right and runs parallel to the waterline. At 1.6 km (1.0 mi), the dike first turns left and then right again. Shortly after, the trail passes a gravelly slope on the left, there is a large depression on the trail that tends to be wet. Beyond that, the trail ascends gently and leads into the woods, obstructing the view of the marshes. The trail continues on this old woods road and hiking is quite pleasant.

At a clearing where the trail continues left, there is a nice view of the New Horton Marsh on the right, and beyond is the hamlet of Upper New Horton with its pic-

Eastern Shores

turesque white church on top of a hill. At 4 km (2.5 mi), the trail makes a 90-degree turn to the right. Here a dike runs parallel to the trail on the right and a fenced marsh lies to the left. The dirt road leaves the marshes and ascends into the woods at 4.5 km (2.8 mi). You should turn around at this point and return to the trailhead as the dirt road continues for only a short distance, ending in a private driveway next to a house on Highway 915.

Trail Features: This trail allows views of the seacoast on one side and marsh areas inland. The New Horton Marsh is a wildlife area that is owned and managed by the Canadian Wildlife Service in conjunction with the Province of New Brunswick. The dikes have been built by Ducks Unlimited. The ecosystem of the wetlands supports a large number of waterfowl. Ducks and herons are commonly seen; dragonflies are also abundant. As their plentiful droppings suggest, the wooded sections are home to coyotes and black bears.

SHEPODY NATIONAL WILDLIFE AREA

Length: 14.8 km (9.2 mi) rtn
Type: linear
Difficulty: easy
Ascent: negligible

Hiking Time: 4 hrs rtn
Map: 21 H/10 Alma
Trail Condition: dry, mostly wide

Access: From Alma, near Fundy National Park, take Highway 114 east. After 14.7 km (9.1 mi), turn right onto Midway Road. Cross the covered bridge and follow the road for 100 m/yd. The trailhead is located at the second path to the left (the first is a private drive-

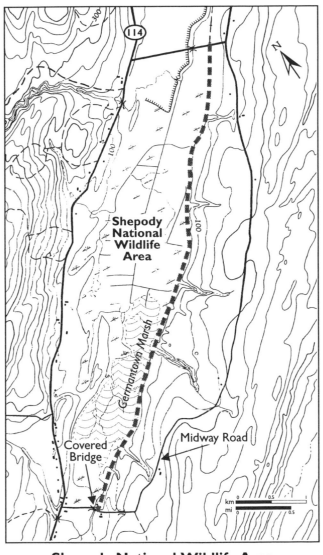

Shepody National Wildlife Area

way) beyond the bridge. There is a blue sign that says "No Vehicles." Four or five parking spaces are found just up the road on the left side opposite a house.

Trail Markings: None, but the trail follows wide, old railway tracks and cannot be missed.

The Trail: The trail leads through shady woods, passing a picnic table and a pit toilet. To the left there are some views of Germantown Marsh, but vigorous young growth generally obstructs the view along the first part of the trail. At 2 km (1.2 mi) the trail continues through an old field. Ruffed grouse are common in this area, and there are frequent views of the marsh on the left. Boardwalks cover some muddy areas, but damage has been done to the trail and the wooden boardwalks and bridges by four-wheelers. The trail passes a field close by another old homestead, and at 7.4 km (4.6 mi) it ends at a country road.

Trail Features: The trail combines the rich wildlife of the Germantown and Beaver Brook Marshes, owned by Ducks Unlimited, with that of the forest. Ducks, geese and herons are seen, as are grouse. Lucky hikers may even see a black bear or a moose, though they're more likely to find only tracks or droppings. Wildflowers and old apple trees can be seen in the fields along the way along with spotted touch-me-nots and the ubiquitous cattails in the marshes.

MARYS POINT PENINSULA

Length: 6.5 km (4 mi)
Type: loop
Difficulty: moderate
Ascent: 50 m (150 ft)

Hiking Time: 2 hrs 15 min
Map: 21 H/10 Alma
Trail Condition: rocky, slippery, impassable at high tide

Access: From Riverside-Albert, take Highway 915 in a southerly direction for 3.5 km (2.2 mi) to Harvey. Turn left and follow the road, which is first paved and later dirt (in good condition), for 4 km (2.5 mi). The visitor centre of the Marys Point Shorebird Reserve is located on the left side of the road. A small parking lot can accommodate four vehicles, and additional parking is available alongside the road.

Trail Markings: The trail is unmarked, but it is not difficult to find.

The Trail: The narrow path starts next to the visitor centre where information on bird migration is available. It descends and soon reaches a fork, signed "Salt Marsh" to the left and "Beach" to the right. The salt marsh section is a short spur that crosses a field, descends to the marsh, continues the loop on a long boardwalk section, and then returns to the fork. The main trail continues to the beach.

Note: From mid-July to the end of August, the trail ends here. The reason is the tens of thousands of shorebirds, mostly semipalmated sandpipers that congregate here to feed on tiny mud shrimps and worms in preparation for their long flight south. Bird-watching is best during the first two weeks of August at low tide. Also note that hikers cannot proceed beyond the beach during high

Marys Point. H.A. EISELT

tide. Furthermore, vehicles of any kind are not allowed on the beach.

At the beach, turn left and continue along the shore-line. Walking along the beach is usually slow and tiring. Keep the wooded section of Marys Point to the left. Eventually, the beach swings to the right and gets rocky. At the tip of the peninsula there is plenty of rockweed on the rocks, which makes walking slippery. Some scrambling is required to get around a big slanted rock. Beyond that, there are more rocks until you reach a seastack. From here, a lighthouse becomes visible on neighbouring Grindstone Island.

Continue along the rocky shore until you see a large slab near the high water line. Here a wide, grassy trail leads steeply into the woods. It soon levels off and turns right. From here, walking is easy. The trail continues through dense woods and descends. Once you are out of the woods, turn right towards the northern beach.

After reaching the beach, turn left and keep to the right of the wooded sections of the peninsula. Orientation is easy; note that the beach from where the birds can be observed is located slightly to the left of a large green field near the trailhead. From this beach the trail returns to the trailhead.

Trail Features: The main features of this trail are the unique plants, crustaceans and shorebirds in the ecosystem of beach and mudflats.

CAPE MARINGOUIN

Length: 5.2 km (3.2 mi) rtn
Type: linear
Difficulty: easy
Ascent: 30 m (100 ft)

Hiking Time: 1 hr 15 min rtn
Map: 21 H/10 Alma
Trail Condition: wet spots

Access: Take Highway 106 west out of Sackville. Turn south onto Highway 935 towards Wood Point and Rockport. Follow this road (first paved, later gravel) for 18 km (11 mi). Continue straight into a dead-end road as Highway 935 turns right at a 90-degree angle. After 7.4 km (4.4 mi) the road ends at a primitive turnaround at Slacks Cove on the left. The trailhead is straight ahead.

Trail Markings: The first part of the trail is unmarked but obvious. Later it narrows and is indicated with some blue marking tape.

The Trail: The wide trail leads into the woods, passing a camp on the right and later one to the left. The trail

Eastern Shores

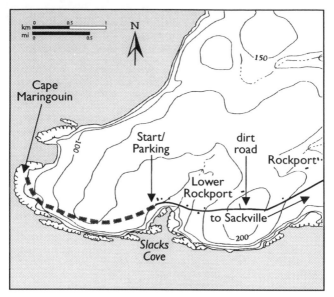

Cape Maringouin

then passes an area of young growth and continues on a gentle downward slope to a fork at 1.8 km (1.1 mi). The left fork is a 200 m/yd side trail leading to a spectacular cliff. The main trail continues straight for another 400 m/yd, where you may enjoy another fine view from Cape Maringouin across the Shepody Bay. Here the narrow path turns right. It ends after another 400 m/yd at a cliff overlooking a small cove.

Trail Features: The key features of this trail are the spectacular cliffs and the beautiful views across Shepody Bay.

WESTCOCK MARSH

Length: 5.3 km (3.3 mi)   **Hiking Time:** 1 hr 30 min
Type: loop   **Map:** 21 H/10 Alma
Difficulty: easy   **Trail Condition:** dry
Ascent: negligible

Access: Take Highway 106 in a southerly direction out of Sackville and turn left onto Highway 935 towards Wood Point and Rockport. Follow this road for 1.6 km (1 mi), and, as it swings to the right, continue straight on to a gravel road. Follow this road for 2 km (1.2 mi) to its end at a dike. The trail starts here.

Trail Markings: None, but the trail is obvious.

The Trail: On the dike, turn left and continue along the dike. Note Fort Beauséjour towards the east at the edge of the Fort Cumberland Ridge. At low tide you can see the remarkable red clay of the Cumberland Basin with its tidal inlets. At 2.4 km (1.5 mi) a trail departs to the left, next to a barn. Continue on the dike for another 1.4 km (0.9 mi), then leave the dike to the left at another barn. Continue on until you reach a T-junction. Turn left, and in 1 km (0.6 mi) you reach the trailhead.

Trail Features: The trail features include some fine views across the fields, marshes and tidal flats south of Sackville.

Eastern Shores

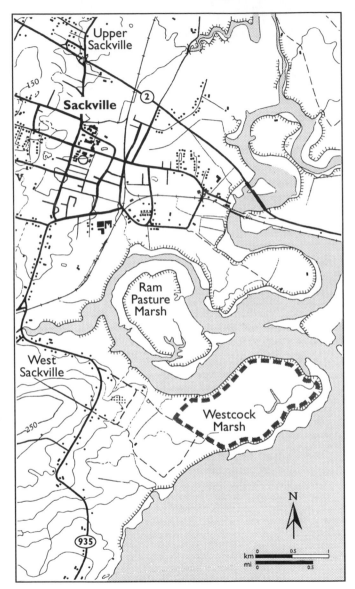

Westcock Marsh

SACKVILLE WATERFOWL PARK

Length: 2 km (1.2 mi)   **Hiking Time:** 30 min
Type: loop   **Map:** 21 H/10 Alma
Difficulty: easy   **Trail Condition:** dry,
Ascent: negligible   mostly boardwalk

Access: From the Trans-Canada Highway (Highway 2),
take exit 541 towards Sackville to a chimney on the left
side of the street. The trailhead is located next to the
smokestack. There is ample parking space on the other
side of the street next to the octagonal tourist information centre.

Trail Markings: None, but this nature walk cannot be
missed.

The Trail: The wide, gravelly trail leads into the park,
until a side trail departs to the left. Take this side trail
and follow a boardwalk with a number of interpretive
signs. At a fork, a spur to the left continues to a T-junction. The trail the right leads to a wooden observation
tower that provides good views across the park, while
the trail to the left leads to a picnic area. Back at the
fork, continue to a T-junction at a gravel path. Turn right
and immediately left again. The trail continues on a
boardwalk until its end near a stand of cattails, where it
leads up to East Main Street, near St. Paul's Anglican
Church. Turn right and return to the parking lot, about
500 m/yd from here.

Trail Features: The major attraction of this self-guiding
nature trail is the large variety of plants and birds typical
of the wetlands. Interpretive signs identify birds and
plants and explain wetland formations and the habitats
they provide.

PAUNCHY LAKE

Length: 6 km (3.7 mi) rtn
Type: loop
Difficulty: easy
Ascent: negligible

Hiking Time: 1 hr 30 min rtn
Map: 21 H/16 Amherst
Trail Condition: generally dry

Access: From the Trans-Canada Highway (Highway 2), take exit 541 near Sackville. Turn onto Highway 940 north towards Midgic. Follow that road for 2.7 km (1.7 mi) to a stone bridge, turn right immediately beyond the bridge, and turn left at a nearby fork. Follow this road for 1.2 km (0.7 mi). Turn right onto High Marsh Road, cross a covered bridge and follow this gravel road for 9.7 km (6 mi). At this point, a gravel road departs to the right, and a smaller road departs to the left. Park the vehicle here alongside the road, or turn left and follow the very rough dirt road through the Tintamarre National Wildlife Area for 2.7 km (1.7 mi) to Paunchy Lake. We describe the trail from the lake.

Trail Markings: None, but the trail is obvious and cannot be missed.

The Trail: The grassy trail continues straight ahead, keeping Paunchy Lake to its right at a distance. It follows a creek or canal to its right through meadows. After some distance, the trail swings to the right and parallels a canal to its left. On the left, a stand of dead tamaracks can be seen. At 1.8 km (1.1 mi), the trail turns left, continuing between two marshy lakes. In this area, waterfowl is abundant. Continue straight at a fork until you reach a T-junction. Turn left for 0.5 km (0.3 mi) and left again for another 1 km (0.6 mi). This part

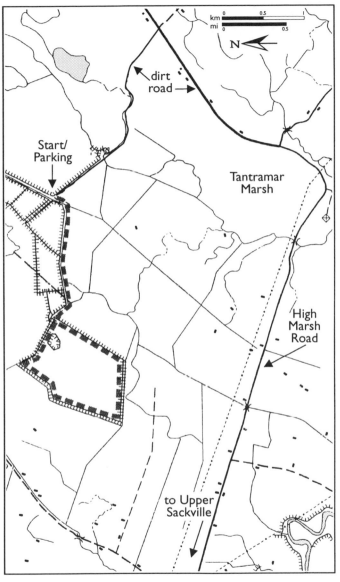

km
mi

N

dirt
road

Start/
Parking

Tantramar
Marsh

High
Marsh
Road

to Upper
Sackville

Eastern Shores

Paunchy Lake

Sackville Waterfowl Park. H.A. EISELT

of the trail continues on top of dikes that are badly overgrown. At a T-junction, you reach the main trail again; turn right and return to Paunchy Lake.

Trail Features: There is abundant waterfowl in all the marshes. Of particular interest in this area are the black ducks. Along the access road to the lake, note a plaque describing the support of Ducks Unlimited, the Province of New Brunswick, the Canadian Wildlife Service and Massachusetts sportsmen in managing this area. There are several blinds in the area for hunting and observing wildlife.

DOBSON TRAIL
(in 7 sections)

Length: 58.4 km
(36.5 mi) one way
Type: linear
Ascent: 330 m (1,100 ft)
Difficulty: moderate

Maps: 21 H/2 Moncton,
21 H/15 Hillsborough,
and 21 H/10 Alma
Hiking Time: 3 days
one way
Trail Condition: mostly
dry, some wet areas

Summary:

Section 1: 9.6 km (6 mi)
Section 2: 5.1 km (3.2 mi)
Section 3: 10.9 km (6.8 mi)
Section 4: 6.8 km (4.2 mi)
Section 5: 6.5 km (4.1 mi) [+ 1 km (0.6 mi) rtn]
Section 6: 9.4 km (5.7 mi)
Section 7: 10.6 km (7 mi)

Access: The trailhead is located south of Moncton on Pine Glen Road in Riverview. From Moncton, take the causeway across the Petitcodiac River and turn left (east) onto Highway 114. In Riverview, turn right onto Pine Glen Road just behind an Ultramar station. Proceed for 3.1 km (1.9 mi). The trailhead is indicated by a sign on the right side of the road at a large parking space.

The trail-end can be reached by entering Fundy National Park on Highway 114, at its northwest entrance near Wolfe Lake. About 1.2 km (0.7 mi) south of the park entrance, the Old Shepody Road departs to the left. Follow this gravel road for 10.9 km (6.8 mi). The end of the Dobson Trail is located a short distance beyond Haley Brook. At this point, the trail connects with the Laverty Falls Trail on the right. A big white sign on the left shows the end of the Dobson Trail. A potential parking space is found by driving up the logging road on the left for about 100 m/yd.

Trail Markings: The trail is marked by blue 6" x 2" plastic blazes or equivalent paint blazes. Some earlier markings are white and very light blue. In some places, distances (in km) are shown on brown wooden plates. Mileages are also sometimes displayed between two horizontal green bars. In general, one blue blaze marks the trail. Two blue blazes, one above the other, indicate that the trail changes its direction. Green blazes mark side trails. In some areas, large numbers of red paint blazes mark the trees; they indicate boundaries and claim lines and can be ignored. It must be pointed out that in some areas, especially those with recent logging activity, the blazes may not be obvious: some markings are found on rocks and on tree stumps. At times, blue marking tape may be used. Caution: follow the blue blazes at all times, because the Dobson Trail frequently leaves the larger trails (e.g. old woods roads) and continues on smaller footpaths!

Section 1: PINE GLEN ROAD TO BEAVER POND. The trail starts at the far end of the parking lot. It leads through mature mixed woods until it reaches a power line at 0.9 km (0.6 mi). The trail crosses the clearing and, under the second of the three power lines, leaves the well-defined path and turns slightly to the left onto a smaller foot path, which is marked by some light-blue blazes on rocks. Once the trail is back in the woods, the blazes are again clearly visible. Mill Creek can sometimes be seen to the right of the trail.

At 1.6 km (1 mi), the trail reaches another clearing with power lines. Underneath the second power line, a smaller footpath departs to the left of the larger trail.

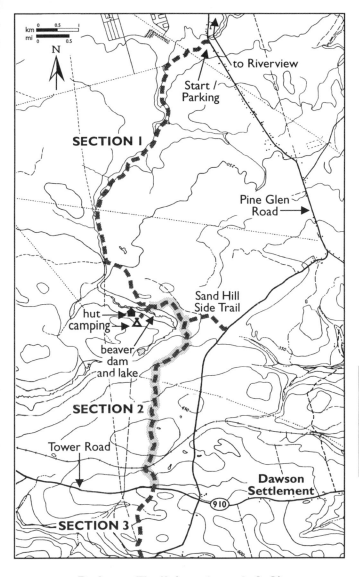

Dobson Trail (sections 1, 2, 3)

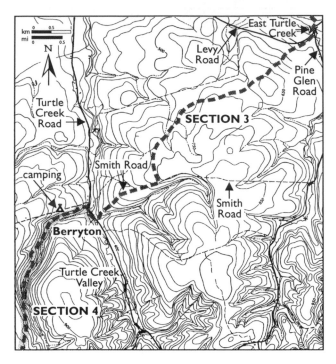

Dobson Trail (sections 3, 4)

Follow this small path. The following section consists of relatively young growth, mostly softwoods. Mill Creek is still to the right of the trail. A wilderness campsite appears after the trail crosses a few small brooks. The trail continues straight until it crosses another brook at 4 km (2.5 mi). Right after the crossing, the trail turns left, ascends rather steeply for a short while, and then turns right at a 90-degree angle.

At 6.1 km (3.8 mi), the trail reaches a partially overgrown clearing with power lines. Keeping the creek to the right, cross the clearing parallel to the creek. The trail enters the woods immediately above the creek.

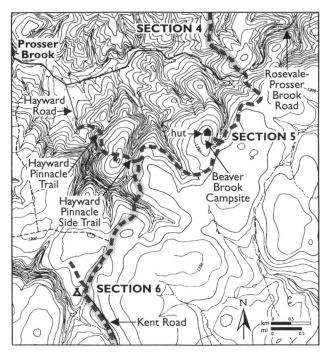

Dobson Trail (sections 4, 5, 6), Hayward Pinnacle

After a short distance, the trail joins an old woods road. From here on the Dobson Trail meanders about this woods road, alternating repeatedly from its right to its left.

At some point a meadow becomes visible to the right. Pass a sign saying "8 km," turn off onto a woods road, and turn right into the woods where the main road takes a 90-degree left turn. There is a beaver pond on the right with beautiful sheep laurels along its edge. At 9.4 km (5.9 mi), a wider road is reached. Turn right and immediately left again. (The trail that continues straight crosses a dam to a wilderness campground and

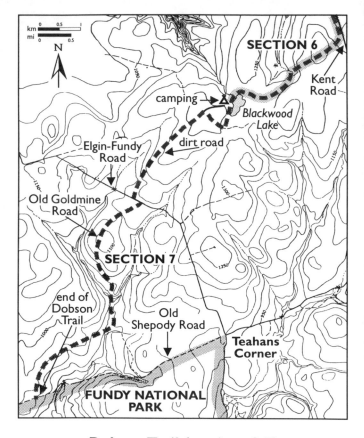

Dobson Trail (sections 6, 7)

hut. Caution should be exercised when crossing the dam as many of its logs are loose and rotten.)

Section 2: BEAVER POND TO TOWER ROAD. The trail continues on the east side of the pond. Just after the trail crosses a small end section of the swamp meadow (called Mill Creek Meadows), it reaches a junction at 10.2 km (6.2 mi). Here the Sand Hill Side Trail leaves to the left and connects with the paved Pine Glen Road. This access trail is marked by two parallel green blazes and is 1.3 km (0.8 mi) in length. It is quite pleasant to hike, if you disregard the illegal dumping site near Pine Glen Road.

The main path swings to the right just beyond the junction, turns left shortly after, crosses Mill Creek, and continues through softwoods in a southwesterly direction. At 11.9 km (7.4 mi), it reaches a gravel road with the Hillsborough power lines just beyond. The trail continues beyond the power lines slightly to the right. The walking is swampy, even though there are some logs across wet spots. Finally the trail ascends and at 12.6 km (7.8 mi) there is a beautiful big pine tree in the middle of the trail. Hiking through the open hardwoods is excellent in this area.

A sometime pond on the right of the trail is passed, and at 14.3 km (8.9 mi) the trail reaches the tracks of the CN railway. The trail follows the tracks to the left in an easterly direction for some 200 m/yds, then it turns right into the woods. The hiking is good until you reach Tower Road at 14.8 km (9.2 mi).

Section 3: TOWER ROAD TO BERRYTON. Cross Tower Road and reach a clearing with young growth at 15.8 km (9.8 mi). Proceed through softwoods, and after a steep descent you reach an old woods road. Turn left onto that road; it dips down and reaches the paved Pine Glen Road at 16.6 km (10.3 mi). Turn right onto that road and proceed across the culvert over East Turtle Creek. This is a good spot to replenish your drinking water. It is also a popular fishing spot. About 50 m/yrd beyond the bridge, Levy Road leaves to the right. The trail follows this road for about 300 m/yd and then it enters the woods to the left at a sign saying Dobson Trail just as Levy Road swings right. At first, the trail leads through nice hardwoods. (At one point, a short side trail leads to a spring, which tends to degenerate to a mud puddle in summer.) Hiking is good here with some possible sites for camping.

At 20.5 km (12.7 mi), the main trail descends to Woodmouse Brook and follows it for a while. Smith Road is reached at 22.4 km (13.9 mi). The trail turns right and follows this dirt road for about 3.2 km (2 mi) all the way down to Berryton. Some raspberry and blackberry bushes as well as birch and maple trees line the road. At one point, you are rewarded with a scenic view onto the opposite hill across the Turtle Creek Valley. At 25.4 km (15.8 mi) the trail reaches the paved Turtle Creek Road at the hamlet of Berryton. Turn right and soon after cross a bridge across Turtle Creek. Here is a good opportunity to replenish your supply of drinking water.

Section 4: BERRYTON TO ROSEVALE-PROSSER BROOK ROAD. Walk across the Berryton bridge and immediately turn left, parallel to Berryton Brook. The trail soon reaches a gravel pit. Enter the gravel pit and continue on the far left (not straight) where the trail enters the clearcut. Join a wide trail and turn left. Proceed through a logging area, then mixed forest with good walking. At 26.6 km (16.5 mi) the trail crosses a brook, and, after a short and relatively steep incline, it turns left, away from the woods road. This part of the trail crosses a number of small brooks and there are a few wet spots. Despite some steep ascents, hiking through the beech and maple trees is pleasant. At a clearcut at 29.8 km (18.5 mi), the Dobson Trail turns left. The trail passes a sometime pond to the right, and at a T-junction it turns left. There are a few old campsites in the area. At 31.6 km (19.6 mi) along this excellent trail section you are rewarded with fine views towards the Prosser Brook ridge and across the wooded Stuart Mountains. The trail reaches the gravelly Rosevale-Prosser Brook Road at 32.5 km (20.2 mi).

Section 5: ROSEVALE-PROSSER BROOK ROAD TO HAYWARD PINNACLE. The trail crosses the Rosevale-Prosser Brook Road and climbs up on another gravel road for some 300 m/yd straight ahead, where it enters the woods on the right. The trail steadily gains altitude before dipping down twice to brooks. Apart from many roots and rocks on the trail, the hiking here is quite good through mostly hardwood ridges.

At 34.9 km (21.8 mi), a little footpath branches off to the right. It leads to the Beaver Brook campsite; the hut provides shelter and a nice view across the nearby pond. Continuing on the main trail, which is an old logging road, walking becomes very wet, even in summer. A new path has formed on higher ground to the right of the woods road. At 35.6 km (22.1 mi), the road turns sharply to the right and soon crosses Upham Brook. The crossing is followed by a short but steep ascent. After that, the trail climbs again and keeps to the right. It is somewhat difficult to follow in this area. The mossy trail then levels off and continues through dark softwoods, and it later swings to the left and reaches a T-junction at 38.6 km (24 mi). The trail continues on an old, wide woods road to the left.

Turning to the right leads to Hayward Pinnacle. The Hayward Pinnacle side trail is marked by green paint blazes. The short 1 km (0.6 mi) round trip to the hilltop is a main attraction of the Dobson Trail and definitely worthwhile. Follow the woods road for about 300 m/yd and then turn left onto a narrow path that is a bit obscured in places. The short, steep path leads to the summit of Hayward Pinnacle. From this, the highest elevation in Albert County, the vista is quite impressive. Towards the north-northeast, you can see parts of Moncton, and towards the northwest the hamlet of Prosser Brook is visible. The views in the other directions are partly obscured by large trees. Return to the T-junction. (Note: The distance for this side trail is not included in that of the Dobson Trail. Also note that the Hayward Pinnacle can be reached from Prosser Brook.)

Section 6: JUNCTION OF HAYWARD PINNACLE SIDE TRAIL TO BLACKWOOD LAKE. From the junction at the Hayward Pinnacle Side Trail, continue on the woods road until 39.2 km (24.4 mi), when the trail leaves the woods road to the right. This path is partially overgrown, but the area is beautiful. Hayward Brook provides another place to stock up on water. Turn right and bypass an old log bridge. The trail briefly follows an old logging road and then turns right into the woods. After a short incline, it crosses a woods road. At 40.8 km (25.5 mi), the trail crosses another woods road and reaches a clearing just beyond. The trail continues for some 200 m/yd with the cutover section to its left. Just before it reaches a little hill, the trail crosses a clearing. For some time the trail leads through young stands of maples and beeches with some undergrowth.

At 42.4 km (26.5 mi), the trail reaches Kent Road. (From here, a short side trip leads to a number of good campsites at the site of an old homestead. To reach the campsites, turn right onto Kent Road for 100 m/yd; they are located on the left-hand side.) The main trail continues left on Kent Road and follows it for 1.8 km (1.1 mi) to a sign saying "Dobson Trail," where the trail turns right into the woods. (Note the raspberry bushes on the right side of Kent Road – a good snack in August!)

The wide woods road provides easy hiking but soon gets rocky. There are some nice old fields with tall grass and goldenrod. This section between Kent Road and Blackwood Lake is very scenic, alternating between woods and old fields. The trail turns right at a junction, with good hiking through a hardwood ridge, and continues on an old, grassy road until it reaches the shores of Blackwood Lake at 48.4 km (30 mi). This is a good camping and rest area. The lake also provides a plentiful supply of drinking water.

Section 7: BLACKWOOD LAKE TO OLD SHEPODY ROAD AT FUNDY NATIONAL PARK. The trail continues straight, with the Blackwood Lake to its left. At the far end of the lake, the trail crosses a wide dirt road leading to the right. The trail continues straight and becomes grassy, partially overgrown, and sometimes wet. It soon swings to the right, and after about 250 m/yd the path turns sharply to the right and arrives at a cairn with a blue blaze facing the dirt road.

At this point, the trail turns left onto the road and follows it for about 2.5 km (1.6 mi), where it ends at a T-junction with the Elgin-Fundy Road. Turn left onto this road for a very short distance and turn right again onto the Old Goldmine Road. Pass a new cabin; at 54 km (33.6 mi) the remains of an old homestead can be seen in the middle of a pretty field of tall grass and goldenrod. The Old Goldmine Road enters the woods and becomes grassy.

The trail passes a campsite, crosses Broad River, and continues straight ahead. Keep left at a fork. The trail then climbs for some time. Cross a wide gravel road with a brook on the left and continue straight. Right after, the trail crosses a creek, ascends through beautiful hardwoods, and reaches a logging road at 56.9 km (35.4 mi). From here, it is possible to proceed in one of two ways.

A) Turn right for about 50 m/yd and then turn left into the woods. Here the trail leads through dense brush. At

57.9 km (36 mi), you reach an open area. Here the trail is marked by orange flags as well as white stakes with blue tops. Continue straight across the clearing. While the view across Fundy National Park and the surrounding hills is nice, walking is extremely rough over uneven terrain, tree stumps, logs and wet spots. Cross this rugged area in a southwesterly direction until you reach a logging road. Turn left onto that road for a short while, as far as the junction of the Old Shepody Road (the Fundy Park boundary) at 58.4 km (36.5 mi). You have now reached the end of the Dobson Trail. From here it is possible to continue on the Laverty Falls Trail in Fundy National Park.

B) This is an alternative (and easier) route to the end of the trail. Turn right onto the logging road and follow it for 0.9 km (0.6 mi). At the T-junction, turn left onto another logging road. This leads 1.3 km (0.8 mi) to the end of the Dobson Trail at the Old Shepody Road.

Trail Features: This 59 km (37 mi) footpath from Riverview to Fundy National Park is the work of many volunteers under the direction of trail master Edwin Melanson. As you would expect, a trail of such length offers a wide variety of scenery. This includes a hilltop with a panoramic view, a wilderness lake, beaver ponds, hardwood ridges, views, and fields that contain old homesteads with raspberry and blackberry patches as well as a multitude of wildflowers. Wildlife includes all large New Brunswick game animals: deer, moose and black bears.

Camping: Hikers may tent at large or at any of the suggested sites. Tenting or making fires at the edge of the trail is discouraged. Hikers should move off the trail for at least 30m (100 ft).

Campfires: From April 21 to October 21, hikers must obtain permits if they intend to make campfires along the trail. These permits are availabe free of charge from the N.B. Forestry Service, P.O. Box 33, Hillsborough, N.B. E0A 1X0, phone (506) 734-2376, or any other branch of the Forestry Service in New Brunswick. For that purpose, hikers must specify hiking dates, sections of the trail that are going to be hiked, as well as the number of hikers in the party. As with tent sites, the site of a campfire should be at least 30 m to 60 m (100 ft to 200 ft) away from the trail.

Water Supply: Streams are an excellent source of drinking water. They are recommended over marked springs, which are frequently muddy or dried out in summer. For instance, the East Turtle Creek at 16.6 km (10.4 mi), Turtle Creek in Berryton at 25.4 km (15.9 mi), and Upham Brook at 36.6 km (22.9 mi) are free-flowing streams that carry drinking water. The water in the lakes and ponds can also be used. It is strongly recommended, however, to use a water filter or purifying tablets for water taken from these sources.

Toilet Facilities: There are no pit toilets on the trail. Dig a hole at least 15 m (50 ft) from the trail and bury excrement and toilet paper 15 to 20 cm (6 to 8 inches) deep so that they can decompose fairly quickly and out of sight.

Eastern Shores

HAYWARD PINNACLE

Length: 4.2 km
(2.6 mi) rtn
Type: linear
Difficulty: moderate to
strenuous
Ascent: 225 m (750 ft)

Map: 21 H/15
Hillsborough,
also Dobson Trail map
Hiking Time: 1 hr 30 min
rtn
Trail Condition: rocky spots

Access: From Moncton, take the Trans-Canada High-way (Highway 2) in a southwesterly direction. At Petitcodiac take the Highway 905 east about 8 km (5 mi) to Pollett River. Continue to Parkindale and turn right at the Parkindale general store. Follow the road for about 5.5 km (3.4 mi) to Prosser Brook. Turn right onto Hayward Road. The trailhead is marked by a sign for the Dobson Trail and is located 0.8 km (0.5 mi) into Hayward Road on the left. Some parking spaces can be found on a field a little farther down the road to the left.

Trail Markings: The trail is marked by green blazes, which indicate that this is a side trail of the Dobson Trail. The two trails connect, but this is a very nice trail in its own right.

The Trail: The trail immediately ascends at a rather steep grade. It reaches a junction with a woods road at 0.5 km (0.3 mi), where it turns right. The trail levels off but soon continues to ascend through maples and beeches. It levels off again, and at 1.9 km (1.2 mi) a smaller path departs to the right for the summit. The short and rocky trail goes steeply upward until it reaches the summit.

Trail Features: The main feature of this trail is the panoramic view from Hayward Pinnacle, the highest elevation in Albert County. In addition to the pastoral scenery around Prosser Brook to the northwest, Moncton may be seen to the north-northeast.

CENTENNIAL PARK LOOP

Length: 4 km (2.5 mi)
Type: loop
Difficulty: easy
Ascent: negligible

Hiking Time: 1 hr
Map: 1:7,500 map from Community Services, City of Moncton
Trail Condition: dry, groomed and lighted trail

Access: Approaching Moncton on Highway 15, take the St. George Boulevard exit. Follow St. George Boulevard for 1.5 km (0.9 mi) and turn left just behind the display of a locomotive and an airplane in front of a car dealership, both on the left side of the street. Follow the road for about 1.2 km (0.75 mi) to its end at a gate, just before the road makes a 90 degree left turn. Park the vehicle alongside the road.

Trail Markings: Cross-country ski trails are permanently marked with yellow, orange, and green blazes. We follow the orange trail which is lighted throughout, making it easy to follow.

The Trail: The trail passes through the gate, enters the woods straight ahead, and immediately turns left at a sign with a map. At this point, the green, orange, and yellow trails all follow one wide shared trail through mixed woods. At some point, the green trail departs to the left, and the yellow trail later turns off to the right. Pass a football field to the right. Shortly after, all three trails join again. Cross Jonathan Brook and follow it for a while, keeping it to the right. When the trail leaves the woods and ends at a wide dirt road, turn to the left. Follow this road to the bend at the trailhead.

Trail Features: A pleasant city forest with some nice hardwood stands and a small brook.

BUCTOUCHE SANDBAR

Length: 22.6 km (14.2 mi) rtn
Type: linear
Difficulty: easy to moderate
Ascent: negligible

Hiking Time: 6 hrs rtn
Maps: 21 I/10 Richibucto and 21 I/7 Buctouche
Trail Condition: dry, sandy

Access: From Miramichi, follow Highway 11 in a southerly direction. Take exit 32B-A and drive 0.8 km (0.5 mi) towards Bouctouche. There Highway 134 swings to the left, but Highway 475 continues straight. Follow Highway 475 for 9.2 km (5.7 mi), then, across from a snack bar, turn right onto a short dirt road that ends not far from the beach. There is plenty of parking. The trail follows the beach.

Trail Markings: None, but as the trail follows a sandbar, it cannot be missed.

The Trail: The trail has recently been blocked off to ATV's, but hikers can walk along the beach close to the waterline. After 1.8 km (1.1 mi), the trail passes a defunct jetty. At 10.8 km (6.8 mi), the beach turns sharply

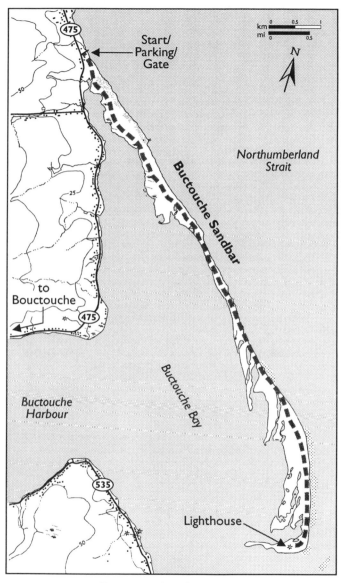

Start/
Parking/
Gate

km
mi

N

Northumberland
Strait

Buctouche Sandbar

to
Bouctouche

475

Buctouche
Harbour

Buctouche Bay

535

Lighthouse

Buctouche Sandbar

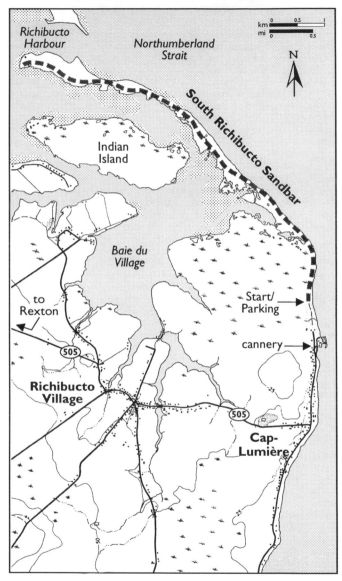

Richibucto Harbour

Northumberland Strait

km

mi

N

South Richibucto Sandbar

Indian Island

Baie du Village

to Rexton

505

Start/ Parking

cannery

Richibucto Village

505

Cap- Lumière

South Richibucto Sandbar

to the right (west). After a short distance, a lighthouse marks the end of the trail. From here, there are some fine view points across the Bay of Buctouche.

Trail Features: Many shore birds can be seen along the beach. Some shells and an occasional sand dollar may also be found.

SOUTH RICHIBUCTO SANDBAR

Length: 17.2 km
(10.8 mi) rtn
Type: linear
Difficulty: easy
to moderate
Ascent: negligible

Hiking Time: 4 hrs rtn
Map: 21 I/10 Richibucto
Trail Condition: dry, sandy

Access: From Moncton, follow Highway 11 in a northerly direction. Take exit 53 at Rexton/Big Cove, and turn right onto Highway 505 towards Cap Lumière. Follow this road for 14.2 km (8.8 mi) to a T-junction at the Northumberland Strait. Turn left and follow the road for 2.4 km (1.5 mi), passing a cannery on the way, to its end at a primitive turnaround. The last part of the road is no longer paved, but it is still passable.

Trail Markings: None, but as the trail follows a sandbar, it cannot be missed. An easy rule for this trail is, "If in doubt, keep left."

The Trail: At the far end of the turnaround, descend to the beach but keep to the left. The trail follows a grassy road that allows good views across the marshes towards Indian Island and the mainland. The trail passes two shacks at 4.8 km (3 mi) and another couple of cabins at 7.7 km (4.8 mi). After that, the trail soon reaches the beach. From here, you can either retrace your steps or swing to the right and follow the beach. North Richibucto Beach can be seen across the Richibucto Gully.

Trail Features: A large number of shore birds, including the rare piping plovers, can be observed along the quiet sandbar.

POINT ESCUMINAC BEACH TRAIL

Length: 12.4 km (7.8 mi) rtn	**Hiking Time:** 2 hrs 30 min rtn
Type: linear	**Map:** 21 P/2 Point Escuminac
Difficulty: easy	
Ascent: negligible	**Trail Condition:** depends on tide

Access: From the Chatham bridge, follow Highway 117 south for 59.2 km (37 mi). Just past a wharf, Escuminac Provincial Park is located on the left side of the road. There are plenty of parking spaces, some picnic tables and two pit toilets. The trailhead is located on the beach beyond the dunes.

An alternative approach is to take Highway 11 from Moncton in a northerly direction. Take exit 75 and follow Highway 117 through Kouchibouguac National Park to Escuminac. At a T-junction in Escuminac, turn right and continue for 3.2 km (2 mi) to Escuminac Provincial Park.

Trail Markings: None, but the trail follows the beach and cannot be missed.

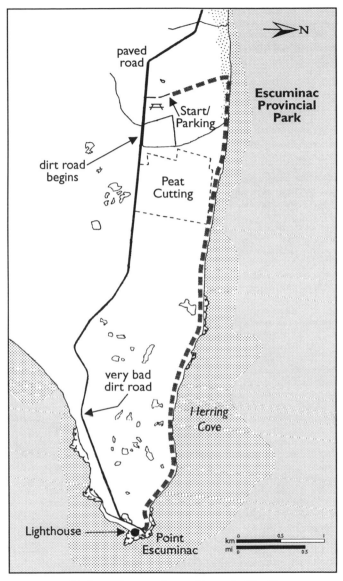

N

paved
road

**Escuminac
Provincial
Park**

Start/
Parking

dirt road
begins

Peat
Cutting

very bad
dirt road

Herring
Cove

Lighthouse → Point
Escuminac

km
mi

Eastern Shores

Point Escuminac Beach Trail

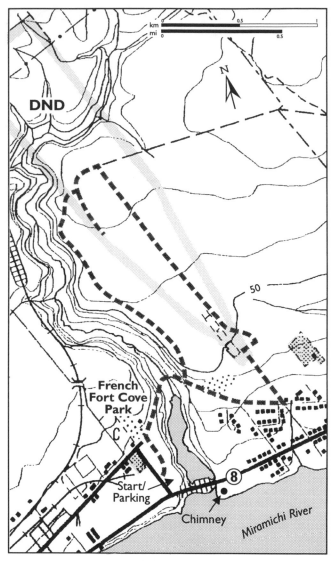

French Fort Cove Trail

The Trail: Once you reach the wide Miramichi Bay, turn right (east) and follow the wide sandy beach. A little further, the sand dunes to the right of the beach are replaced by peat moss. As the miles pass, the beach gets narrower and more gravelly, and the peat moss "cliffs" become higher. Towards the end of the trail, these bluffs are 3 to 4 m (10 to 12 ft) high. Sheltered in the little coves, the tides have deposited broken lobster traps, buoys, pieces of rope, netting and shells. Just below the modern Point Escuminac Lighthouse, the shore turns into a plateau of shale. The trail ends at the lighthouse.

Trail Features: The beach is lined with sand dunes that gradually change to spectacular peatmoss cliffs. Beachcombing is good in the coves formed by these cliffs, particularly for old lobster traps and buoys.

FRENCH FORT COVE TRAIL

Length: 6.4 km (4 mi)   **Hiking Time:** 1 hr 30 min
Type: loop   **Map:** 21 P/4 Sevogle
Difficulty: easy   **Trail Condition:** dry
Ascent: 30 m (100 ft)

Access: Entering Newcastle from the south on Highway 8 (King George Highway), turn left onto Cove Road just before you reach a large chimney on the right side of the road. Coming from the other direction, Cove Road is located in front of a large sign on the right side of the road that bids visitors "Welcome to Newcastle." On Cove Road, turn right onto a parking lot. The trail starts at the far end of the lot.

Trail Markings: The trail is unmarked but easy to follow.

The Trail: The wide, groomed trail leads into the woods. It then swings to the right and descends. It crosses a bridge over scenic French Fort Brook. (For access to French Fort Cove, turn right beyond the bridge.) The trail gets narrower and ascends until it reaches a junction; turn left just before it reaches the junction. Hiking is quite spectacular in this area with the steep gorge on the left and cliffs on the right. The path then turns to the right and continues through a burnt-over area where the forest is slowly recovering. The trail eventually turns from a northerly to an easterly direction, and soon after reaches a T-junction. Turn left and soon the trail swings to the right at a 90-degree angle. After a while it reaches a 4-way junction. Keep to the right. The grassy trail continues in a southerly direction, passes a tree farm, and then leads through a stand of mature aspen. Ignore a narrow path that turns off to the right, and continue straight through a small gravel pit. Soon after, you reach a ball park on the left of the trail. Here a narrow path turns off to the right, crosses a field in a westerly direction and, as it reaches the end of the field, turns left into the woods. A few minutes later, the trail reaches a wide woods road. Turn left and follow the road to a subdivision. Turn right onto French Fort Road and continue straight back into the woods. Stay on the wide trail, which descends to French Fort Brook, crosses it, and returns to the parking lot the same way it came.

Trail Features: This trail includes a good view across a gorge and access to a quiet cove as well as a walk along a forest recovering from a major fire.

In 1755, a battery was built at French Fort Cove for the protection of Acadians who had fled here after their expulsion from Nova Scotia. It was later levelled by British troops.

LITTLE SHEEPHOUSE FALLS NATURE TRAIL

(Miramichi Pulp and Paper Co.)

Length: 0.8 km (0.5 mi)   **Hiking Time:** 30 min
Type: loop   **Map:** 21 P/4 Sevogle
Difficulty: easy   **Trail Condition:** dry,
Ascent: negligible   groomed trail

Access: From Highway 8 near Miramichi, take exit 415 north to Red Bank and follow the road for 9 km (5.6 mi). Turn left onto Highway 420 and cross the bridge over the Miramichi River to Sunny Corner. Go straight/left directly beyond the bridge and follow the road for 0.5 km (0.3 mi), then turn left onto Highway 425 at a Stop sign at the ranger station. Follow the road for 19.3 km (12 mi) and turn left onto Highway 430 towards Heath Steele. Continue for 4.2 km (2.6 mi) to the junction with Fraser Burchill Road, where a wooden sign already indicates the trail. Turn left onto Fraser Burchill Road (a good gravel road). Follow it for 10.1 km (6 mi), and turn left again onto Little Sheephouse Road at a wooden sign. Continue on this road, crossing a small bridge along the way until you reach a fork at 4.5 km (2.8 mi). Keep left and proceed for another 2.5 km (1.6 mi). The trailhead is located on the left side of the road at a small picnic site just before a bridge. There is space for about 10 vehicles.

Trail Markings: None. This is a groomed nature trail that is easy to follow.

Trail Features: This nature trail has a number of explanatory plaques pointing out features of various species of softwood, animal life, facts about glaciation, and the legend of Sheephouse Brook. Of specific interest is the trunk of a 350-year-old white pine, displayed at the trailhead.

KOUCHIBOUGUAC NATIONAL PARK

Kouchibouguac National Park, one of New Brunswick's two national parks, was established in 1969. With its 240 km^2 (92 mi^2), it is the largest park in the province. The name "Kouchibouguac" derives from a Micmac word meaning "river of the long tides." This park differs dramatically from Fundy, the province's other national park. It is flat, and its major attractions are salt marshes, the seashore, sand dunes, bogs and beaches, with their marine environment. Due to the Labrador Current, the water in the Northumberland Strait is quite chilly; in contrast, the water temperature in shallow lagoons may reach 20°C (68°F) in July and August.

The park offers a wide variety of outdoor recreation, most prominently biking, canoeing and hiking. Bird-watching is also excellent along the shore and in the marshes. Interpretive programs conducted by rangers are also offered.

Accommodation in Kouchibouguac National Park is available in two campgrounds: South Kouchibouguac campground with 219 sites, and the slightly more primitive Côte à Fabien campground with 32 sites, some of them of the walk-in kind. In addition, there are three primitive campsites: Petit-Large with eight sites, and Sipu and Pointe-à-Maxime with four sites each. The Petit-Large site can be reached on foot and by bike; Sipu is accessible by foot and by canoe, and Pointe-à-Maxime by canoe only.

Kouchibouguac National Park is reached from Moncton by taking Highway 11 and following it for 91 km (57 mi). Turn right onto Highway 480, cross Highway 134, and enter the park. Continue straight to a junction with the visitor centre located on the right. The trailheads of all trails in the park are described from this junction.

Three topographical maps are needed to cover the entire area of Kouchibouguac National Park: 21 I/14 Kouchibouguac, 21 I/15 Pointe-Sapin, and 21 I/10 Richibucto. Hikers are, however, served a lot better by buying the Kouchibouguac National Park map, which shows all trails. It is available at the visitor centre. For more information on the park, call (506) 876-2443.

TWEEDIE TRAIL

Length: 1.2 km (0.7 mi) **Hiking Time:** 20 min
Type: loop **Map:** Kouchibouguac
Difficulty: easy National Park Map
Ascent: negligible **Trail Condition:** dry

Access: From the junction at the visitor centre, continue straight on Highway 117 north for about 3.2 km (2 mi). The trailhead is located on the right side of a parking lot.

Trail Features: The main features of this trail are a saline marsh, a cattail marsh and wildflower fields on the shores of the Kouchibouguac River. It is advisable to stay on the gravel trail, as poison ivy grows among the raspberries, thistles and fireweed.

OSPREY TRAIL

Length: 5.1 km (3.2 mi) **Hiking Time:** 1 hr 15 min
Type: loop **Map:** Kouchibouguac
Difficulty: easy National Park Map
Ascent: negligible **Trail Condition:** dry

Access: From the visitor centre, continue north on Highway 117 for about 6.7 km (4.2 mi), then turn right onto the dirt road towards the Loggiecroft/Côte à Fabien shore. Follow this road for 4 km (2.5 mi), then turn left to the Côte à Fabien shore campsite. After 300 m/yd the road makes a sharp right turn. The group campsite is located straight ahead, and that is where the trail starts.

Trail Markings: Unmarked, but cannot be missed.

The Trail: Pass the gate and follow the boundary of the group campsite on the left. Once the trail reaches the Kouchibouguac Lagoon, it turns sharply to the left and soon enters the woods, with the lagoon always visible on the right. Walk around an inlet with a log jam, and at 1 km (0.6 mi) keep right at a junction towards Black River Point. At 1.6 km (1 mi), we recommend the side trail to the right that leads to a sandy beach at Black River Point. Many sea and shore birds can be observed in this area. Back at the T-junction, the trail continues straight through a small stand of tall softwoods until, at 3.9 km (2.4 mi), it reaches the junction where the loop began. Turn right and return to the trailhead at the group campsite.

Trail Features: The main feature of this trail is the many shore birds that can be observed along the beach. Particularly prominent are the great blue herons, ospreys and the abundant terns.

CLAIRE FONTAINE TRAIL

Length: 3 km (1.8 mi)   **Hiking Time:** 50 min
Type: loop   **Map:** Kouchibouguac
Difficulty: easy   National Park Map
Ascent: negligible   **Trail Condition:** dry

Access: From the junction at the visitor centre, continue on Highway 117 north for 9.2 km (5.7 mi). There is no sign, only a small parking lot on the right just before you cross the Black River. The trailhead is located at the far end of the parking lot.

Trail Markings: None, but the trail is obvious.

The Trail: After leading through a field for a short distance, the trail soon enters the woods and reaches a fork. Take the right fork, which is nicely lined with sweet fern, bayberries and blueberries. The forest gets gradually denser. At about 0.9 km (0.5 mi), Rankin Brook can be seen to the right of the trail. Following the brook, the trail reaches the tip of the peninsula, and returns along the south bank of the Black River. At 2.6 km (1.6 mi), the trail leaves the river and swings to the left. Shortly after, it leads through tall grass and raspberry bushes before returning into the woods. Back at the fork, turn right and return to the parking lot.

Trail Features: A nice forest trail with views across Rankin Brook and the delta of the Black River.

Eastern Shores

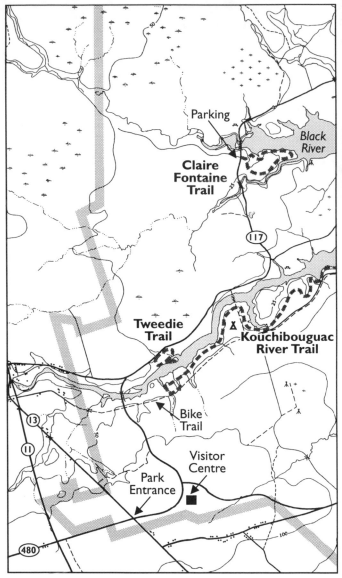

Parking

Black River

**Claire
Fontaine
Trail**

117

**Tweedie
Trail**

**Kouchibouguac
River Trail**

Bike
Trail

13

11

Visitor
Centre

Park
Entrance

480

Kouchibouguac

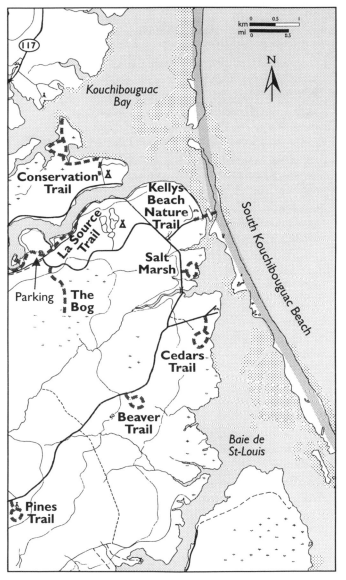

National Park

PINES TRAIL

Length: 0.8 km (0.5 mi)   **Hiking Time:** 15 min
Type: loop   **Map:** Kouchibouguac
Difficulty: easy   National Park Map
Ascent: negligible   **Trail Condition:** dry

Access: Turn right at the visitor centre towards "Beaches" and follow that road for 3.5 km (2.2 mi). The trailhead is at the parking lot on the right side of the road.

Trail Features: A nice nature trail through the woods, with a fine stand of eastern white pines, among them an impressive 40 m (130 ft) white pine.

BEAVER TRAIL

Length: 1.4 km (0.9 mi)   **Hiking Time:** 25 min
Type: loop   **Map:** Kouchibouguac
Difficulty: easy   National Park Map
Ascent: negligible   **Trail Condition:** dry

Access: Turn right at the visitor centre towards "Beaches" and follow that road for about 6.8 km (4.2 mi). Parking is available at the right side of the road.

Trail Features: As the name of this self-guiding trail suggests, the work of the beaver is its main feature. An inactive beaver pond is at the centre of the raised boardwalk trail.

CEDARS TRAIL

Length: 1 km (0.6 mi)   **Hiking Time:** 15 min
Type: loop   **Map:** Kouchibouguac
Difficulty: easy   National Park Map
Ascent: negligible   **Trail Condition:** dry

Access: Turn right at the visitor centre towards "Beaches" and follow that road for 9 km (5.6 mi), then turn right onto a dirt road towards Callanders Beach. After 0.9 km (0.6 mi), the road ends in a loop, circling a picnic area. The trailhead is on the right side of the road where it reaches the loop. There is some parking space on the left.

Trail Markings: None. Once the trailhead has been found, the trail is fairly obvious.

The Trail: The trail crosses the field, passing the remains of an old homestead. It then enters the woods and continues on a boardwalk lined with cedars and maples. At 0.6 km (0.4 mi), the trail reaches St. Louis Lagoon. It then swings around and returns to the trailhead.

Trail Features: These include a raised boardwalk loop with interpretive signs. The scenery consists mostly of woods and a glimpse of the seashore.

Eastern Shores

SALT MARSH

Length: 0.8 km (0.5 mi)
Type: loop
Difficulty: easy
Ascent: negligible

Hiking Time: 15 min
Map: Kouchibouguac
National Park Map
Trail Condition: dry,
boardwalk

Access: Turn right at the visitor centre towards "Beaches" and continue on that road for about 9.9 km (6.2 mi). There is a parking lot on the right side of the road.

Trail Features: An "open book" display explains some of the major features of this salt-marsh nature trail. Of particular interest are the different types of grass that grow close to or farther away from the waterline, depending on their salt-tolerance. Great blue herons may be seen in the marsh.

KELLYS BEACH NATURE TRAIL

Length: 1.4 km
(0.9 mi) rtn
Type: linear
Difficulty: easy
Ascent: negligible

Hiking Time: 30 min rtn
Map: Kouchibouguac
National Park Map
Trail Condition: dry,
boardwalk

Access: Turn right at the visitor centre towards "Beaches" and continue on that road for about 10.8 km (6.7 mi). There is a large parking lot straight ahead. The trail starts at the canteen to the right of the parking lot.

Trail Features: This nature trail follows the boardwalk towards the beach. It leads through a number of different ecosystems. The saltmarshes and dunes are of particular interest. Some "open book" displays along the trail explain a number of local features. Note the marram grass that stabilizes the dunes. Kellys Beach, at the end of the trail, is a beautiful sandy beach that is supervised daily during the summer months.

THE BOG

Length: 2 km
(1.2 mi) rtn
Type: linear
Difficulty: easy
Ascent: negligible

Hiking Time: 40 min rtn
Map: Kouchibouguac
National Park Map
Trail Condition: dry

Access: Turn right at the visitor centre towards "Beaches" and follow that road for about 18.4 km (11.4 mi). A parking lot is located to the left of the road. The trailhead is at the far left of the lot.

Trail Features: A spiral-staircase observation tower provides a very good view across the bog. Among other plants, bakeapple (also called cloudberry), cottongrass and black spruce are rather prominent.

LA SOURCE TRAIL

Length: 2.6 km
(1.6 mi)
Type: loop
Difficulty: easy
Ascent: negligible

Hiking Time: 50 min
Map: Kouchibouguac
National Park Map
Trail Condition: dry

Access: Turn right at the visitor centre towards "Beaches" and follow that road for 14.5 km (9 mi) to its end. Parking is available at a picnic site. The trailhead is located at the far right of the parking lot.

Trail Features: The trail features include a large field where once an old homestead was located. There are also some good views across the Kouchibouguac River, where benches invite you to stay for a while. Of special interest is the hanging red pine tree at Sandstone Gardens. Here you may turn back on the same trail or return on the nearby bicycle trail.

KOUCHIBOUGUAC RIVER TRAIL

Length: 16.8 km (10.4 mi)
Type: loop
Difficulty: easy to moderate
Ascent: negligible

Hiking Time: 4 hrs 30 min
Map: Kouchibouguac National Park Map
Trail Condition: dry, a few wet spots

Access: Turn right at the visitor centre towards "Beaches" and follow that road for 18.8 km (11.5 mi) to its end. Parking is available at a picnic site. The trailhead is located just past the kitchen shelter and water pump.

Trail Markings: None in this direction, but with one exception the trail is easy to follow.

The Trail: The 1 m (3 ft) wide trail starts to the right of a wide bike trail. The trail soon reaches the Kouchibouguac River, which it follows for about 11 km (6.8 mi). At 1 km (0.6 mi), it reaches a T-junction. The short side trail to the right leads to a bench overlooking the river; turn left to continue on the shady main trail. After a while the trail crosses a small bridge, from which the work of beavers can be seen to the left. A little farther on it crosses another bridge with more signs of beaver activity. The trail passes a marshy inlet, and at 5.8 km (3.6 mi) it reaches a T-junction. The left fork connects to a bike trail; the right fork continues the hiking trail.

Beyond that junction the trail becomes narrower. Keep right at a beaver dam and cross the dam, which may be slippery. At 7.8 km (4.8 mi), the trail reaches the primitive Sipu campground. Sipu is located to the right of the trail and has four picnic tables, barbecue pits, pit toilet, wood supplies, a water pump and access to the Kouchibouguac River. Shortly beyond Sipu, the trail leads through a beautiful small stand of tall softwoods. At 9.1 km (5.7 mi), the trail is partially obscured by dense raspberry patches, and beyond that point it is a little overgrown. The trail then turns sharply to the left, leaves the Kouchibouguac River and soon reaches a wide bike trail. At this point, you can either retrace your steps or turn onto the bike trail and follow it for 5.8 km (3.6 mi) back to the shelter.

Trail Features: There are some good views across the Kouchibouguac River. Shore birds, especially herons, and cormorants may be seen along the trail. The vegetation along the trail is lush. Raspberries and mushrooms may be found in season.

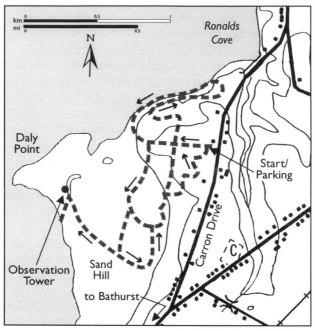

Daly Point Reserve Nature Trail

DALY POINT RESERVE NATURE TRAIL

Length: 5 km (3.1 mi)   **Hiking Time:** 1 hr 15 min
Type: loop   **Map:** 21 P/12 Bathurst
Difficulty: easy   **Trail Condition:** dry,
Ascent: negligible   boardwalk

Access: Approaching Bathurst on Highway 11 Bypass towards Caraquet, take exit 300A. Continue on Miramichi Avenue (Highway 134 north). Cross some railroad tracks and, at the second traffic light, turn right onto Bridge Street. Follow it for 2.4 km (1.5 mi), then turn left onto Carron Drive. After another 1 km (0.6 mi), the parking lot of the Nature Reserve is located on the left side of the road.

Trail Markings: The trails are marked by different theme names as shown on the local trail map that is available at the visitor centre.

The Trail: The trail starts in front of the visitor centre, where it turns left and continues on a wide road, passing two pit toilets on the way. Here the "White Pine" path departs to the left; this is where the trail returns later. This trail continues straight. A short distance ahead, the smaller "Coastal Trail" departs to the right. Follow this woodchip-surfaced path through aspen. The trail stays high on the cliffs with the shore visible on the left below. At a junction, turn right into the woods onto "Gulch Path." The path skirts the gulch and returns on a boardwalk and wooden steps to the beach. Walk along the beach for some 400 m/yds where the beach swings to the right, turn inland onto a wide, grassy trail. At a junction, turn right onto "Saltmarsh" (trail #2 on the local map). Just before a raised boardwalk with cattails, there is a shortcut to the left along the "Woodland Trail"; our trail, however, continues straight. It soon reaches an observation tower. Here you are rewarded by a nice view across the bay and towards nearby Bathurst.

Return on the boardwalk and bear to the right at a fork onto the "Warbler Trail." Follow the trail through alders, and turn right at a T-junction. After a short distance, turn right onto the narrow "White Pine Path" which leads back to the visitor centre.

Trail Features: The park consists of a salt marsh and old fields an mixed forests. The nature trail gives visitors an opportunity to identify and view plants and animals.

Special attractions include the Canada geese that arrive on their migratory route in the fall and the rare maritime ringlet butterfly. Daly Point Reserve is a joint venture of Brunswick Mining and Smelting Corp. Ltd. and the New Brunswick Department of Natural Resources and Energy.

APPALACHIAN HIGHLANDS

APPALACHIAN HIGHLANDS

The Appalachian Highlands, of which New Brunswick's Sugarloaf and Mount Carleton provincial parks are part, is the most remote area of the province. Its colonial history began with a visit from Jacques Cartier at the Bay of Chaleur in 1534. The French settled along the shore and the mountains in 1690, and during the 1800s the British came, mostly settlers from Scotland and Ireland.

The region is dominated by densely forested highlands. At Mount Carleton, the highest elevation in the Maritimes, the vistas are spectacular. The Restigouche River is famous for its Atlantic salmon.

The forests are the region's riches, and lumbering is one of the major industries. In addition, there are a number of maple groves near Kedgwick and St. Quentin where maple syrup is produced.

Appalachian Highlands

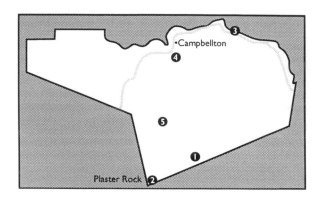

BIG BALD MOUNTAIN TRAIL

Length: 11 km (6.8 mi) rtn
Type: linear
Difficulty: moderate
Ascent: 240 m (800 ft)

Hiking Time: 2 hrs 45 min rtn
Map: 21 O/1 Big Bald Mountain
Trail Condition: Some mud holes

Access: On Highway 8 near Miramichi, take the exit towards Red Bank on Highway 415 and follow this road for 9 km (5.6 mi). Turn left onto Highway 420, follow the river, and eventually cross the bridge over the Miramichi River to Sunny Corner. Go left/straight directly beyond the bridge and follow the road for 0.5 km (0.3 mi), then turn left onto Highway 425 at a Stop sign at the ranger station. Follow Highway 425 for 1.9 km (1.2 mi) to a junction at the sign saying "Back Road." Turn left, cross the bridge, and immediately after, leave the Back Road and turn right onto the Mullin Stream Road. This new dirt road is in very good condition. It turns to the left behind two big drums and continues for about 20 km (12.5 mi) until it is joined from the right by the South Sevogle River Road. After a short distance, keep right at a fork and continue on the South Sevogle River Road. After about 21 km (13 mi), Slacks Lake Road departs to the right. Stay on the main road, pass a modern-day lumber camp on the left side of the road, and continue for about 12.5 km (7.8 mi). Watch for two iron posts and a boulder to the right of the main road.

Turn right off the main road and continue straight, first up a small hill, then level. Ignore a road to the right, and later one to the left (which leads into a clearcut). The road swings to the right; ignore two turnoffs to the right, and turn left at a huge rock on the left side of the road. Continue for 1.5 km (0.9 mi), and park at a small turnaround just before reaching a clearcut. The trailhead is located on the far right of the turnaround. There is parking space for about eight vehicles.

Trail Markings: None. The trail follows woods roads and is easy to follow.

The Trail: Walk down an old woods road to the right of the parking space. The trail is nicely lined with birch trees. Just after reaching the bottom, bypass a mud hole on the left. Another water hole can be bypassed on the left across a beaver dam. The trail now leads through a very pretty open area, lined with scattered hardwood trees, sheep laurel and Irish moss. At 1.6 km (1 mi), the trail reaches an intersection with the foundation of a collapsed cabin on the left. Turn left onto a wide sandy woods road. This road is often used by ATVs.

A system of large mud puddles can be bypassed on the left by using tracks made by four-wheelers. The heavily eroded trail now starts to ascend. The trail levels off at a plateau, then descends at a gentle grade. It then swings to the right into more mature softwoods and levels off briefly before it begins to climb. Ignore the turnoff to the right and follow the main road straight ahead. The summit of Big Bald Mountain is reached at 5.5 km (3.4 mi).

Trail Features: The main feature of this trail is the panoramic view from the top. Unfortunately, litter and vandalism are problems, specifically on the summit. Along the trail, partridges are frequently seen.

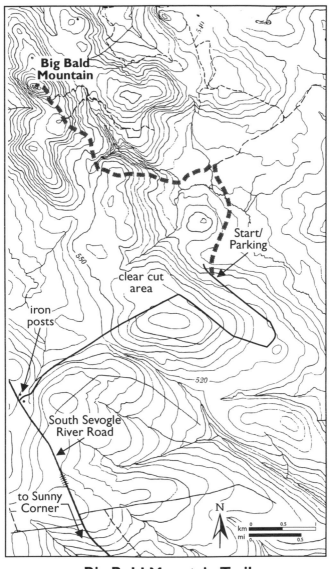

Big Bald
Mountain

Start/
Parking

clear cut
area

iron
posts

550

520

South Sevogle
River Road

to Sunny
Corner

N

km 0   0.5   1
mi 0   0.5

Big Bald Mountain Trail

Big Bald Mountain Trail. H.A. EISELT

SADLERS NATURE TRAIL
(Plaster Rock Tourist Park)

Length: 1.7 km (1.1 mi)   **Hiking Time:** 30 minutes
Type: loop   **Map:** 21 J/14 Plaster Rock
Difficulty: easy   **Trail Condition:** groomed,
Ascent: negligible   dry

Access: From the south of the province, take the Trans-Canada Highway (Highway 2) in a westerly direction towards Edmundston. Exit the highway at Perth-Andover, and follow Highway 109 towards Plaster Rock. Cross the Tobique River and turn right onto Highway 390. The Tourist Park is located on the left side of the road just before the turnoff of Highway 385.

Trail Markings: None, but the trail is impossible to miss.

The Trail: From the parking lot, follow the sign "Nature Trail" to a turnaround. The woodchip-surfaced nature trail turns off to the left, leads around Roulston Lake, and returns to the turnaround.

Trail Features: At various points the trail gives access to the lake and its ecosystem.

CHARLO DAM LOOP

Length: 6.3 km (3.9 mi)   **Hiking Time:** 1 hr 30 min
Type: loop   **Map:** 21 O/16 Charlo
Difficulty: easy to   **Trail Condition:** dry
moderate
Ascent: 30 m (100 ft)

Access: From Campbellton, take Highway 11 in an easterly direction. Take exit 385 to Charlo. Turn right at a Stop sign and follow the road for 0.8 km (0.5 mi). Turn left onto Morris Street, towards Charlo Airport, and follow this road for 1.6 km (1 mi). Turn right onto Charlo Dam Road just before you enter the premises of the airport. Follow this road for 1.3 km (0.8 mi) to a Stop sign. Turn left and immediately right at a sign saying "Adventure Chalet." Follow the dirt road to a cabin where another road joins from the right. There is parking for about 20 vehicles.

Trail Markings: None, but the trail is obvious and should not be missed.

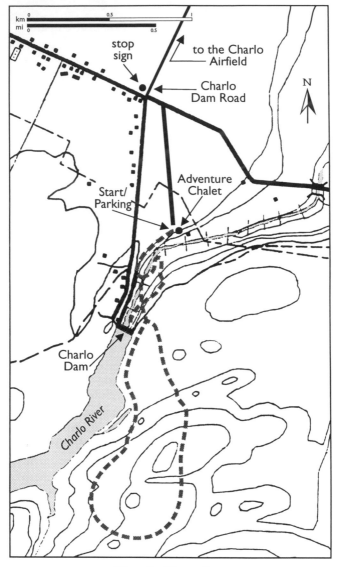

Charlo Dam Loop

The Trail: Pass the small cabin and walk down the wide dirt road to the chalet of an outdoors club. Continue past the main house and a few smaller buildings. The trail keeps the Charlo River to its left and passes a cascading mountain brook to its right. The trail crosses Charlo River on a bridge and turns immediately to the right. The loop starts here. At a T-junction, the main trail departs to the left. (We recommend hiking the short distance to the right to Charlo Dam. The wide trail ends just below the large dam. Note the wooden pipeline on the other side of the river. The adventurous hiker may climb up the very steep hill next to the dam to have an overview of the reservoir.)

The main trail climbs and soon reaches a T-junction. Turn right and keep left at a fork. Do not take the trail that leads backwards! The wide trail passes lots of raspberry bushes and continues through mature mixed forest. There are quite a few short climbs and descents. At 4 km (2.5 mi), the trail turns to the right. Next, keep left at a fork. Another trail joins from the right, and after a while you reach the junction you passed earlier above Charlo River. Then keep left at a fork and continue straight at the next junction. Turn left at another 4-way junction and descend to the bridge, which is where the loop ends. From here, return to the chalet and the parking lot.

Trail Features: The trail follows cross-country ski trails through mixed forest and provides easy access to a dam. The Charlo River and a cascading, mossy brook are also quite scenic.

SUGARLOAF PROVINCIAL PARK

Sugarloaf Provincial Park is located near Campbellton. The park is designed for multiple uses. In addition to a tourist information centre and a picnic area, the park offers lighted tennis courts, an alpine slide and camping facilities. The rather extensive network of trails is shared by joggers and hikers in summer, and skiers and snow-mobilers in winter. The highlight of the park, however, is the summit of Sugarloaf Mountain, from which you have a panoramic view of Campbellton, the Gaspé Peninsula and the Baie des Chaleurs.

The park is easily reached by taking Highway 11 from either St. Leonard or Bathurst. Take exit 415 and follow the signs to nearby Sugarloaf Provincial Park, keeping left twice.

SUGARLOAF SUMMIT TRAIL

Length: 5.1 km (3.2 mi)   **Map:** 21 O/15 Campbellton
Type: loop   **Hiking Time:** 2 hrs
Difficulty: moderate to   **Trail Condition:** dry,
strenuous   groomed trail
Ascent: 240 m (800 ft)

Access: Enter the park and immediately turn left. Cross a bridge and turn left again. There is plenty of parking space available. The trailhead is located at the far end of the lot.

Trail Markings: None, but the trail is well groomed and easy to follow.

The Trail: Follow the wide road to a junction with a memorial honouring Terry Fox. Turn left and follow the

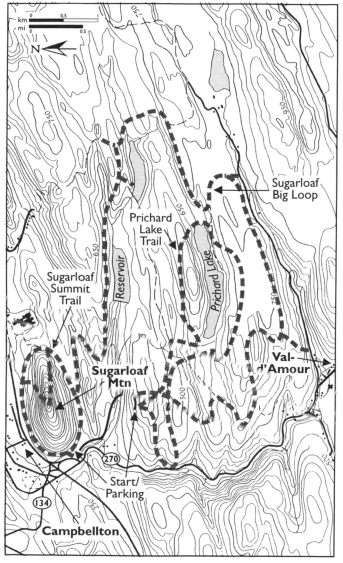

km
mi

N

Sugarloaf
Big Loop

Prichard
Lake
Trail

Reservoir

Prichard Lake

Sugarloaf
Summit
Trail

Val-
d'Amour

**Sugarloaf
Mtn**

Start/
Parking

270

134

Campbellton

Appalachian Highlands

Sugarloaf Mountain

wide gravel road. Just as the road turns right, away from the parallel Highway 11, turn right into the woods onto a narrow path. This small but well-defined path ascends in a westerly direction. Soon the footpath joins a wider trail. Turn right and continue the steep climb with the aid of guardrails and ladders. The trail ascends over boulders and finally reaches Morrissey Rock at the top of Sugarloaf Mountain. A breathtaking view towards Campbellton, the bay (Restigouche Harbour), and the Gaspé awaits the hiker. From here you can return by descending on the wide trail, and then continue on the loop by turning right at the T-junction.

Trail Features: The main feature of this trail is the truly amazing view from the 283 m (929 ft) summit of Sugarloaf Mountain.

PRICHARD LAKE TRAIL

Length: 12.6 km (7.8 mi)
Type: loop
Difficulty: easy to moderate
Ascent: 150 m (500 ft)

Hiking Time: 3 hrs 30 min [+ 30 min side trail]
Map: 21 O/15 Campbellton
Trail Condition: rocky, dry

Access: Enter the park and turn left immediately. Cross a bridge and continue straight towards the campgound. There is a parking lot for many vehicles just right of the entrance to the campground and service road. The trailhead is located next to the service road.

Trail Markings: Part of the trail is marked by 4" x 4" red and green metal blazes, which appear at irregular intervals. We suggest you follow the trail description closely. In winter, this trail is used by cross-country skiers.

The Trail: The wide trail parallels the service road and keeps it to its left. There are a number of connections between the trail and the road. The trail crosses under a power line and ends at the road at 1.8 km (1.1 mi). Turn right onto the road and follow it for about 300 m/yd to a shelter on the left. Directly behind the shelter, the trail descends straight into the woods to the left of a manual pump. Follow the red and green square metal blazes, pass under a power line and follow the sign to Prichard Lake. Soon after, a side trail departs to the right.

This yellow-blazed loop adds about half an hour to the trail, but is very well worth it. Walking here is very enjoyable; the trail is level and leads through hardwoods. At a T-junction, turn left until you reach a junction. This is where the loop ends and reaches the main trail.

If you do not hike the loop, continue straight and reach a T-junction immediately (this is where the loop returns to the main trail). Turn to the left, and a very short distance after you reach a Stop sign. Cross a wide gravel road and continue straight. At another T-junction, turn right onto a fairly wide dirt road. Soon you come to a small picnic site with a table. This site provides the first view of Prichard Lake.

The trail continues around the lake. There are various side trails departing to the right, but the general rule is to keep left. The trail soon enters hardwoods and continues through them for some time. There are no views of the lake. Turn left at a 4-way junction. The trail descends to the lake, located to the left. The trail continues below a pumping station, where it turns away from the lake. Immediately after, turn left at a 4-way

Appalachian Highlands

junction, cross a brook, and ascend through the woods. This red-blazed section is fairly steep. Stay on the main trail, ignoring a smaller side trail that departs to the right. As the trail levels off, there are some red and green blazes. At a junction with a pit toilet, turn right following a sign to X-C Cabin which is the shelter at the trailhead. (Continuing straight at this point completes the loop around the lake, and in another five minutes you reach the picnic spot where the lake first became visible on this trail.)

The grassy trail descends through hardwoods; walking is very pleasant in this section. Turn right at a T-junction towards the shelter onto a wide dirt road. Cross underneath the power lines and reach another Stop sign. Cross a dirt road straight into the woods onto a narrower trail. This trail continues for another 0.5 km (0.3 mi) back to the shelter. From here, return to the campground on the same trail as on the way up.

Trail Features: The trail leads through nice hardwoods and offers some pleasant views of Prichard Lake.

SUGARLOAF BIG LOOP

Length: 18.5 km (11.5 mi) **Hiking Time:** 5 hrs
Type: loop   **Map:** 21 O/15 Campbellton
Difficulty: easy to   **Trail Condition:** dry
moderate
Ascent: 90 m (300 ft)

Access: Enter the park and turn left immediately. Cross a bridge and turn left again. There is plenty of parking space available here. The trailhead is located at the far end of the lot.

Trail Markings: None, but the trail is wide and obvious. In winter, this trail is used by snowmobiles.

The Trail: Walk up to the Terry Fox Memorial and turn right. Follow the trail for about 1 km (0.6 mi), then turn off to the right onto a wide grassy road. Continue straight at a 4-way junction. The trail continues for a few miles to a T-junction. To the right, a side trail leads to the reservoir. Turn left, and after a little while the trail leaves the park at another T-junction. Turn right and cross the edge of a beaver pond. At 7.9 km (4.9 mi), keep right at a fork. The trail crosses under two of the three power lines, then turns off to the right. At this point there is a fine view of Sugarloaf Mountain.

The trail descends and enters the park again, and then swings to the left, crossing the third power line. Keep straight at a fork and reach a 4-way junction at 10.3 km (6.4 mi). Continue straight, following the signs to the X-C cabin. For the next 45 minutes the trail is fairly level through beautiful hardwoods. At one point, a woods road departs to the left towards Val d'Amour. The main trail goes straight and starts to ascend gently. At 15.4 km (9.6 mi), ignore a trail that departs to the right. Shortly after, power lines are crossed and another track joins from the left. Continue straight, turn left onto a short ascent to a Stop sign, and reach a gravel road at 16.6 km (10.4 mi). Turn right onto this road and walk down to the visitor centre. Alternatively, you can walk on a path that parallels the road on its left. Turn right at the visitor centre and return to the parking lot.

Trail Features: The main attractions are the beautiful hardwoods that are found along much of this trail. Particularly remarkable are the stands of tall, straight birch trees. This is a very pleasant trail with a nice scenic view of Sugarloaf Mountain.

Appalachian Highlands

MOUNT CARLETON PROVINCIAL PARK

Mount Carleton Provincial Park was created in 1969 and is by far the largest provincial park in the province. The park boasts the highest elevation in the Maritimes: Mount Carleton stands about 820 m (2,693 ft) high. This altitude is also partly responsible for the comparatively harsh climate; snow can be expected from about mid-October to mid-May. Large game such as moose, bear and whitetail deer are found in the park, even though hunting has been intense in the surrounding areas.

The rivers and lakes in the area provided good transportation routes for the canoes of Indians and early settlers. In the early 1900s, abundant big game and salmon encouraged sportsmen from several different states, particularly from Connecticut, to set up fishing and game camps next to the Nictau and Nepisiguit lakes. Early tracks around Mount Carleton also served as logging roads for spruce, pine and fir trees, which were then hauled to and floated down rivers to nearby sawmills. The creation of Mount Carleton Provincial Park ensures the preservation of the natural beauty of the area and offers enjoyment of the wilderness for all visitors.

Accommodation in the park exists only in the form of camp and trailer sites, apart from the Mount Carleton Lodge & Resort, Inc., (506) 235-1915. There is a drive-in campground at Nictau Lake with 88 campsites, pit toilets, and water from wells. There is also "Headwaters," a backcountry campground with four sites and a pit toilet. Note that gas and groceries are not available in the park. The nearest services are obtainable in Riley Brook and St. Quentin. However, the Mount Carleton Lodge & Resort, Inc., has recently opened its dining room to the general public.

In order to access the park from the south of the province, take the Trans-Canada Highway (Highway 2) in a westerly direction towards Edmundston. Exit the highway at Perth-Andover and follow Highway 109 towards Plaster Rock. Cross the Tobique River and turn right onto Highway 390. In Plaster Rock, turn left just beyond the new Tourist Park onto Highway 385. The small community of Riley Brook provides the last chance to stock up on supplies and gas. From here, the road continues north for 36.6 km (22.7 mi) where it enters the park. After another 3.4 km (2.1 mi), you reach a turnoff to the right with the new visitor centre. All trails are described from here.

Alternatively, visitors from the northwest of the province can exit the Trans-Canada Highway (Highway 2) at St. Leonard. Take Highway 17 in a northeasterly direction and follow it for some 63 km (39 mi) to St. Quentin. In town, turn right onto Highway 180 towards Bathurst. Follow this road for 31.3 km (19.5 mi). Turn right at a sign to Mt. Carleton Provincial Park onto another dirt road and follow it for some 10 km (6 mi) to the new visitor centre on the left side of the road.

Information concerning the park and the condition of its trails may be obtained toll free at 1-800-561-0123.

Appalachian Highlands

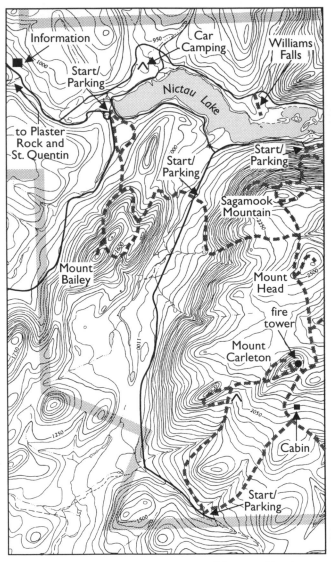

Mount Carleton

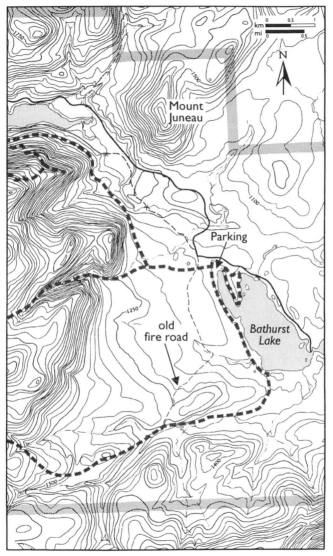

Mount
Juneau

Parking

old
fire road

Bathurst
Lake

Provincial Park

Appalachian Highlands

MOUNT BAILEY TRAIL

Length: 7.5 km (4.7 mi) [+1.6 km (1 mi) side trail to summit]
Type: loop
Ascent: 300 m (1,000 ft)
Difficulty: moderate

Hiking Time: 2 hrs 30 min [+ 30 min to summit]
Map: 21 O/7 Nepisiguit Lakes and park guide
Trail Condition: dry

Access: From the visitor centre, continue in a south-easterly direction for 2.5 km (1.5 mi), passing roads that depart first to the left and then to the right. At a traffic circle with a picnic area on the right, one of the trailheads is located between the second and third road turning off to the right. The trail is described from this trailhead. An alternative trailhead is reached by turning right into the second road (the old Mamozekel Road) and follow it for 0.7 km (0.4 mi).

Trail Markings: The trail is marked by blue metal blazes with a white diagonal bar.

The Trail: From its head, the trail leads immediately into the woods. Keep left; the right forks lead to the group campsite. The trail continues in an easterly direction with Nictau Lake on the left below. The path crosses a short but steep gully and then swings out of sight of the lake. There is a corduroy section across a muddy spot. After a while, the trail starts to ascend gradually towards Franquelin Hill but soon levels off and follows a contour line through mixed forest. This part of the trail is frequently crossed by deer and moose. At 2 km (1.2 mi), the trail turns sharply to the left. It then starts to ascend, first through birch and later softwoods. Keep right at a fork; the trail returns later on the left fork. The trail soon ascends rather steeply for a while. At another junction, it is possible to take the 1.6 km (1 mi) side trail on the right to the summit of Mount Bailey. If at all possible, this "detour" should be attempted. The trail first dips down before it ascends to the summit of 563 m (1,850 ft) high Mount Bailey. Here you have a panoramic view of a mountain range with Mount Sagamook on the left, Mount Carleton straight ahead (clearly identified by its white fire tower on the summit), and Bald Mountain Brook deep below in the valley.

Return to the main trail and turn right. Soon the trail descends and passes through a nice stand of birch trees. As the trail leaves the woods, a 30 m (100 ft) cliff rises right in front of you. At this point, you can either turn left and continue on the main trail or take the detour along the cliffs. Both trails join after about 300 m/yd. The cliff trail, clearly marked by red paint blazes on rocks, continues along the sheer cliffs. Appropriate caution is advised on this short but very spectacular section of the trail. Just beyond the point where the cliff trail turns left and back into the woods, another fine view may be enjoyed with Mount Sagamook on the right and cone-shaped Franquelin Hill straight ahead. The cliff section of the trail turns sharply to the left, descends steeply, and soon joins the main trail.

Continue on the main trail for a little distance, and another short 100 m/yd side trail leads to an observation point. This point, however, offers much less spectacular views than those from the cliff section passed earlier. Some 250 m/yd below this side trail you reach a fork. Keep left to complete the Mount Bailey loop; the right fork marks the start of the Bald Mountain Brook Trail. The main trail (left fork) now descends continuously, and the deciduous forest changes to mixed forest. The path then crosses a small brook and returns to the fork with the "Mount Bailey" sign, where it continues

Mount Sagamook. H.A. EISELT

straight. As the trail continues its descent, watch out for the point where it leaves the old woods road. Continuing on the woods road leads to the alternative trailhead at the Mamozekel Road. This latter option is about 0.9 km (0.5 mi) shorter than the trail described here.

Trail Features: Stunning views from the top of Mount Bailey, as well as from the cliff section of the trail, make hiking this trail worthwhile. Deer and moose are occasionally seen, as are partridges near the cliffs.

BALD MOUNTAIN BROOK TRAIL

(from Mount Bailey Trail to Mount Head Trail)

Length: 5.5 km
(3.5 mi) one way
Type: linear
Difficulty: moderate
to strenuous
Ascent: 390 m (1,300 ft)

Hiking Time: 2 hrs one way
Map: 21 O/7 Nepisiguit
Lakes and park guide
Trail Condition: wet spots,
rocky and rooty

Access: This trail connects the Mount Bailey Trail with the Mount Head Trail. In this guide, the Bald Mountain Brook Trail is described from the Mount Bailey Trail. Neither trailhead nor trail-end are accessible by vehicle. The trailhead is located at a fork along the Mount Bailey Trail, a short distance below the end of the cliffs section, and the trail-end is at the Mount Head Trail, about 0.8 km (0.5 mi) south of the summit of Mount Sagamook.

Alternative access from Bald Mountain Brook Road: Hikers who want to use the Bald Mountain Brook Trail in order to access Mount Head Trail without hiking the Mount Bailey Trail can do so by using this alternative access. From the visitor centre, continue in a southeasterly direction for 2.5 km (1.5 mi), passing roads that depart first to the left and then to the right. At a traffic circle with a picnic area on the right, take the third road turning off to the right with a sign pointing to Mount Carleton. After 2.9 km (1.8 mi), just beyond the crossing of Bald Mountain Brook, the road to the Mount Carleton trailhead departs to the right. Follow this dirt road for 1.1 km (0.7 mi). The trailheads of the two sections of the Bald Mountain Brook Trail are located on the left and right side of the road. A few parking spaces exist on the right side of the road.

Appalachian Highlands

Trail Markings: The trail is marked by blue metal blazes with a white diagonal bar.

The Trail: From its head at a fork along the Mount Bailey Trail, the trail takes the right path and then descends in a northeasterly direction through nice hardwoods. The descent soon steepens and the path swings to the east. At one point, the trail passes a huge pine tree, and it soon reaches Bald Mountain Brook. The trail then makes a sharp turn to the right and follows the brook in a southerly direction. After a short distance, the trail crosses Bald Mountain Brook on a long wooden bridge, ascends shortly, levels off, turns sharply to the right, and soon reaches Bald Mountain Road.

Cross the dirt road and continue along the trail on its opposite side. The trail leads through softwoods in a southeasterly to easterly direction. It first ascends gently, later at a steeper grade. It then descends again and reaches an old beaver pond. The trail continues in a southerly direction along the edge of the forest. After crossing a number of branches of a brook, the path turns left into the woods. It then follows the cascading creek upstream.

After passing a scenic waterfall, the ascent gets steeper. The trail crosses the brook (which can usually be accomplished without getting wet feet) and continues in a southerly direction, away from the water. After a relatively short but steep climb, the grade gets gentler as the trail leads through a nice stand of birch trees.

After a while, the trail crosses the brook again. The trail runs parallel to the brook for a while, then it passes through dense softwoods, and later mixed open forests and a small open field, until it reaches the Mount Head Trail.

Trail Features: The key features of this trail are the beautiful waterfalls of the Bald Mountain Brook and an old beaver pond.

MOUNT SAGAMOOK TRAIL

Length: 8.1 km (5 mi) [+ 2.5 km (1.6 mi) side trails]

Type: loop

Ascent: 510 m (1,700 ft)

Difficulty: strenuous

Map: 21 O/7 Nepisiguit Lakes and park guide

Hiking Time: 2 hrs 40 min [+ 1 hr 20 min]

Trail Condition: rocky and rooty

Access: From the visitor centre, continue in a south-easterly direction for 2.5 km (1.5 mi), passing roads that depart first to the left and then to the right. At a traffic circle with a picnic area on the right, take the third road turning off to the right with a sign pointing to Mount Carleton. After 2.9 km (1.8 mi), a dirt road departs to the right towards Mount Carleton. Continue straight for another 2 km (1.2 mi). There are parking spaces for about 25 vehicles. The trailhead is located on the right side of the road.

Trail Markings: The trail is marked by 2" x 2" blue metal blazes with a white diagonal bar.

The Trail: The trail gently ascends on an old, wide logging road for a short distance, where it coincides with the Caribou Brook Trail (see the trail description on page 260.) Soon the Sagamook Trail turns off sharply to the right, and the path ascends steeply through softwoods. At another fork, turn right again, following the sign saying "Mt. Sagamook" (the trail later returns on the left fork). The trail passes over a refreshing spring, and there are already some good views of Nictau Lake and the mountain range behind it. The trail also passes a stand of birch trees. Note some white quartz boulders on and along the trail. The trail continues to climb through alternating stands of birches and softwoods, and at 2 km (1.2 mi) there is a rocky outcrop. Here, the trail is occasionally marked by red paint blazes on the rocks.

After climbing up the rocks for about 200 m/yd, the trail reaches a junction. From here, a 1 km (0.6 mi) (return distance) side trail departs to the right. This side trail leads to two pinnacles that are approached by walking across a jumble of rocks. There are some fine views of Nictau Lake and surrounding areas. The main trail continues straight and ascends before climbing over more boulders. At 2.5 km (1.6 mi), a 100 m/yd side trail leads to the 777 m (2,550 ft) peak of Mount Sagamook. Here you are rewarded by excellent views of Nictau Lake and Mounts Gordon and Juneau to the north and northeast, as well as Mounts Head and Carleton to the south.

Just below the peak of Mount Sagamook, a trail descends steeply in a southeasterly direction. At 3.6 km (2.2 mi), you arrive at a junction to a lookout on a rocky outcrop. The trail descends steadily, and at 4.4 km (2.7 mi) it reaches another junction where a 1 km (0.6 mi) side trail departs to the right. It leads to another panoramic view point, but the path is very steep, and as it is a dead-end, it is necessary to hike back up. The main trail starts descending, first gently, later at a steeper grade. The path is rocky and rooty in this area. It crosses a brook at 7.2 km (4.5 mi). Keep right at a fork, then left, and from here return straight ahead to the parking lot.

Trail Features: The trail follows an old path established in the early 1900s by Admiral Spruance. Mr. Spruance, an ardent sportsman from Connecticut, stayed at the Nictau game and fishing camps. A spectacular view from the peak of Mount Sagamook of Nictau Lake and adjacent mountain ranges makes this demanding hike worthwhile. The old Indian name Sagamook refers to the reflections in the water of Nictau Lake, which are nearly perfect on a clear day.

MOUNT HEAD TRAIL

Length: 4.8 km (3 mi) one way
Type: linear
Difficulty: moderate
Ascent: 120 m (400 ft)

Hiking Time: 2 hrs one way
Map: 21 O/7 Nepisiguit Lakes and park guide
Trail Condition: rocky and rooty

Access: This trail connects the Sagamook Trail and Mount Carleton Trail. It is not directly accessible by vehicle. Its two trailheads are located just below the summit of Mount Sagamook and at the plateau just below Mount Carleton.

Trail Markings: The trail is marked with orange plywood diamonds and squares.

The Trail: The trail starts about 100 m/yd below the summit of Mount Sagamook and leads across boulders in a southerly direction. Once the rocks are crossed, the trail becomes almost level. The path ascends through nice young mixed forest to a junction at 0.8 km (0.5 mi) where the Bald Mountain Brook Trail departs to the right. Continuing straight, the path reaches another junction at 1.8 km (1.1 mi), where a 1.6 km (1 mi) (return) side trail departs to the summit of Mount Head. It passes a clearing with a few dilapidated buildings, continues on the right side of the clearing, and reaches the summit after a short climb. There are some fine views of Mount Carleton and the Nepisiguit Lakes. Back on the main trail, the path leads through softwoods on mossy boulders. Once the trail reaches a mature forest, it turns right at a 90-degree angle. It dips down to Dry Brook and ascends again, before it reaches the junction with the Big Brook – Dry Brook Loop (see the trail description on page 257).

The trail continues straight, ascends, and then swings to the right. The path follows an old cut that was once planned to be a road but was later not developed. The trail passes through mixed forest with a large number of birch trees before it reaches a clearing on a small plateau, just below the steep but short climb to the summit of Mount Carleton.

Trail Features: The trail connects three of the major summits of the park. Views from all peaks are spectacular.

MOUNT CARLETON TRAIL

Length: 9.8 km (6.1 mi) [+ 2.4 km (1.5 mi) side trail]
Type: loop
Ascent: 390 m (1,300 ft)
Difficulty: moderate

Hiking Time: 3 hrs 30 min [+ 45 min for side trail]
Map: 21 O/7 Nepisiguit Lakes and park guide
Trail Condition: rocky near the top

Access: From the visitor centre, continue in a south-easterly direction for 2.5 km (1.5 mi), passing roads that depart first to the left and then to the right. At a traffic circle with a picnic area on the right, take the third road turning off to the right with a sign pointing to Mount Carleton. After 2.9 km (1.8 mi), just beyond the crossing of Bald Mountain Brook, the road to the Mount Carleton trailhead departs to the right. Follow this dirt road for 8 km (5 mi) to its end. On the right, there is a small parking lot for about 10 vehicles and a pit toilet but no drinking water. The trailhead is located at the far left end of the road.

Trail Markings: Most of the trail is marked by blue metal blazes with a white diagonal bar. In areas where the trail leads across rocks, there are red paint blazes on boulders. The side trail is marked by orange plywood blazes and red paint blazes. In general, finding the route is not difficult.

The Trail: The trail first follows a wide, old woods road through mixed woods. It is rocky in parts, but despite that and the gentle but steady ascent, it is good walking. Many birch trees skirt this grassy old road. At 2.8 km (1.7 mi), the trail reaches a fork. Take the left fork, which immediately ascends rather steeply. (The right fork is part of the Big Brook – Dry Brook Loop.) Soon the trail passes a cabin with a picnic table and a very short side trail to a spring on the left. Beyond the cabin, the main trail gets a bit narrower and allows some glimpses of a rocky outcrop in the distance on the left, including the firetower on top of Mount Carleton. At a clearing at 4.2 km (2.6 mi), the trail turns left. (Straight across the clearing is the trailhead of the Mount Head Trail; see the trail description on page 253.) After a short, steep ascent, the trail arrives at the firetower on the summit of Mount Carleton. On a clear day, there are many fine views from the top, including the Nepisiguit Lakes in an easterly direction.

The trail continues behind the firetower on a rocky ridge. This area provides the best views along the trail. The ridge ends at about 4.7 km (2.9 mi), and the trail descends sharply at the south side of the ridge. It then rounds the ridge and swings west. After a while, the trail gets less rocky and rather flat. An alternative trail section through the woods exists. It avoids the rocky and — in high winds — hazardous ridge. It does, however, also miss out on many good views along the trail.

At 6 km (3.7 mi), the hiker passes the "Headwaters" wilderness campground, which consists of four separate campsites. The trail crosses a beaver dam and reaches a fork just beyond the dam. The path straight ahead leads to the parking lot, whereas the right fork starts a 2.4 km (1.5 mi) loop. This rugged side trail ascends to a summit that allows fine views of Mount Carleton and other peaks in the park. It continues through young softwoods along a rocky ridge with good views, then descends, crossing a jumble of rocks, and arrives at 8.4 km (5.2 mi) at a T-junction with the main trail. The left fork leads back to the wilderness campground. Turn right, and soon the trail crosses a creek, which follows the trail on the right. The path winds through a very nice stand of birch trees. It now descends gently but continually. Leaving the creek, the trail continues in a southeasterly direction and ends at the dirt road just north of the parking lot.

Trail Features: Mount Carleton is the highest peak in the Maritime provinces, and on a clear day the views from there are excellent. When the peak and the firetower are blanketed by fog, they appear eerie. Near the

"Headwaters" wilderness campground there are many signs of moose; this is their winter resting place. This area also boasts a very large number of fiddleheads in the spring.

Note: This trail can be shortened by either omitting the 45-minute side loop or by returning from the summit of Mount Carleton on the same trail. The latter option does, however, miss out on a number of good views, especially those from the rocky ridge behind the firetower. Both shortcuts change the difficulty rating of the trail to "easy to moderate."

BIG BROOK – DRY BROOK LOOP

Length: 19.6 km (12.2 mi)
Type: loop
Difficulty: moderate to strenuous if hiked clockwise, otherwise strenuous
Ascent: 420 m (1,400 ft)

Hiking Time: 7 hrs 30 min
Map: 21 O/7 Nepisiguit Lakes and park guide
Trail Condition: a number of wet spots and fords, frequent deadfall

Access: From the visitor centre, continue in a south-easterly direction for 1.3 km (0.8 mi), then turn left. Cross a bridge and follow the dirt road for about 12 km (7.5 mi), where a small road departs to the right. This road ends at a gate, where there are parking spaces for maybe three vehicles. Pass by the gate and walk a short distance to Nepisiguit Lake. The trailhead of Big Brook Trail is located next to the lake on the right side of a grassy area. Right next to the trailhead of Big Brook Trail is also the trailhead of Dry Brook Trail, which is where the trail returns.

Trail Markings: The trail is marked with blue metal blazes with a white diagonal bar. There are also occasional orange plywood blazes.

The Trail: The level trail follows the shore of Nepisiguit Lake through mixed spruce and white birch woods. Note the signs of beaver activity along the trail. Cross two branches of Brown Brook, and at 2.3 km (1.4 mi) the trail turns right at a 90-degree angle and leaves the shoreline. This part of the trail appears to be an old wagonroad, and it passes through softwoods with vigorous young growth. After a while, the trail ascends and the roaring Big Brook can be heard (but not seen) on the left below. At 4.8 km (3 mi), the path reaches a junction with an old fireroad, which departs to the right. It is possible to return to the parking lot on this road.

Continuing straight ahead, the trail soon reaches an area of current beaver activity. Part of the area is flooded. The original trail continues straight through the swamp, and bypassing the area without getting wet feet is generally difficult. Beyond the swampy stretch, the trail climbs for a while and then levels off. There are some muddy spots in this area; fiddleheads are abundant here in the spring. The trail ascends again and allows glimpses of a mountain range on the right (north). At 8 km (5 mi), the trail leaves the woods road and departs to the right. The path goes through softwoods, and there is quite a bit of deadfall on the trail. At one point the trail steeply dips into a valley and climbs immediately after. Then the path descends to a brook, crosses it, and ascends again at a right angle to the brook. After levelling off, the trail continues in a westerly direction. At 9.8 km (6.1 mi), the trail follows a creek for a short distance until it reaches the junction with the Mount Carleton Trail.

Turn right, and after about 400 m/yd you reach a cabin. Opposite the cabin there is a very short side trail to a spring. Beyond the cabin, the main trail narrows and allows some glimpses of a rocky outcrop and the firetower on top of Mount Carleton in the distance. A clearing is reached at 11.2 km (7 mi) and on the left is a side trail to Mount Carleton (see the trail description on page 254).

The main trail (from this point on called Mount Head Trail) continues on the far side of the clearing. Here a sign to Dry Brook indicates the direction. The trail first leads through mixed forest with a large number of birch trees; it then swings to the left and descends further. This part leads along a long and narrow clearing that is partially overgrown. Watch out for the blazes. The path reaches the junction of the Mount Head Trail and the Dry Brook Trail at 12.6 km (7.8 mi) just before the Mount Head Trail crosses a small, rocky ravine.

The Dry Brook Trail departs to the right and immediately descends steeply, keeping the Dry Brook to its left. The path skirts a beaver pond and then turns right into the woods. The path crosses the brook, which remains to the right of the trail for a little while. Note the decorative Siberian dogwood in some of the wet areas. After a while, the trail crosses the brook again. The trail then drops down and turns left to a waterfall. The creek is crossed a number of times, but the path always keeps close to the brook. A beautiful stand of white birch is passed along the way.

Then the trail levels off, and walking gets easier. Notice the extensive work of the beaver. This is also an area in which the hiker's progress is frequently hampered by deadfall. After skirting a number of beaver ponds, the trail swings to the right, keeping Dry Brook at its left and following it for a while — until only the creekbed remains. This gives Dry Brook its name; the

Appalachian Highlands

creek disappears in the gravelly streambed. The path continues through mixed and pure hardwood ridges. Note the turnoff of the Caribou Brook Trail to the left. Continue through some pretty stands of birch trees. The trail then descends into softwoods, crosses a fireroad, and continues straight ahead to the parking lot.

Trail Features: The main attractions of this trail are found along Dry Brook: a series of tumbling waterfalls, beautiful stands of white birch and active beaver ponds.

CARIBOU BROOK TRAIL

Length: 10 km (6.2 mi) rtn
Type: linear
Difficulty: easy
Ascent: 50 m (150 ft)

Hiking Time: 3 hrs rtn
Map: 21 O/7 Nepisiguit Lakes and park guide
Trail Condition: rocky and rooty, a few wet spots

Access: From the visitor centre, continue in a south-easterly direction for 2.5 km (1.5 mi), passing roads that depart first to the left and then to the right. At a traffic circle with a picnic area on the right, take the third road turning off to the right with a sign pointing to Mount Carleton. After 2.9 km (1.8 mi), a road departs to the right. Continue straight for another 2 km (1.2 mi). The Caribou Brook Trail shares its trailhead with that of the Mount Sagamook Trail. Parking spaces are available on both sides of the road for about 25 vehicles. The trailhead is located on the right side of the road.

Trail Markings: The trail is marked by blue metal blazes with a white diagonal bar.

The Trail: For a short distance, this trail coincides with the Mount Sagamook Trail. The latter soon departs to the right whereas the Caribou Brook Trail continues straight ahead, ascending at a gentle grade. The path leads through nice hardwoods and soon levels off. After a while, the trail crosses a number of small mountain brooks in the mixed forest. On several occations, Mount Juneau can be seen through the trees on the left. At 3.1 km (2 mi), the trail descends and crosses a creek. This area may be wet at times. The roaring Caribou Brook can be heard deep below on the left. The trail swings sharply to the right and reaches Caribou Brook at 3.8 km (2.4 mi). The brook must be forded; sometimes a few rocks or a dead log across the stream allow hikers to keep their feet dry.

The trail continues in a southeasterly direction and starts to ascend through mixed forest. Note the unnamed summit to the right (west) of the trail. Finally, at 5 km (3.1 mi), the trail reaches a wooden bridge crossing Dry Brook. Immediately beyond the crossing, the Caribou Brook Trail ends at a T-junction with the Big Brook -- Dry Brook Loop.

Trail Features: This is the only longer trail in the park that is fairly level and easy going. There are some nice hardwood ridges as well as the scenic Caribou Brook.

PINE POINT TRAIL

Length: 2.2 km (1.4 mi) **Hiking Time:** 40 min
Type: loop **Map:** 21 O/7 Nepisiguit
Difficulty: easy Lakes and park guide
Ascent: negligible **Trail Condition:** dry

Access: From the visitor centre, continue in a south-easterly direction for 1.3 km (0.8 mi), then turn left. Cross a bridge and follow the dirt road for about 12 km (7.5 mi), where a small road departs to the right. This road ends at a gate, where there are parking spaces for maybe three vehicles. Pass by the gate and walk a short distance to Nepisiguit Lake. The trailhead of the Pine Point Trail is located next to the lake on the left side of a grassy area behind a log cabin.

Trail Markings: The trail is marked by blue metal blazes with a white diagonal bar.

The Trail: Immediately beyond the trailhead there is a fork. Keep to the right (the trail returns on the left fork) and follow the lakeshore. This area leads through very pretty red pines. The trail then swings left and rounds the tip of the peninsula. Soon the trail enters a beautiful stand of white birches. At this point, some islands are visible to the right. The work of beavers can be observed in this area. The trail ascends gently and returns through softwoods, cutting across this small peninsula. It re-enters the stand of pines and descends to the parking lot.

Trail Features: The pure stand of red pines on the east shore is a main feature of this trail. They are the result of natural reforestation, following the 1933 forest fire. In addition, an attractive grove of white birch and nice views across Lake Nepisiguit make walking this short trail very worthwhile. Listen to the cry of the common loon while you round the peninsula.

WILLIAMS FALLS

Length: 0.6 km
(0.4 mi) rtn
Type: linear
Difficulty: easy
Ascent: negligible

Hiking Time: 15 min rtn
Map: 21 O/7 Nepisiguit
Lakes and park guide
Trail Condition: dry, gravel

Access: From the visitor centre, continue in a south-easterly direction for 2.5 km (1.5 mi), then turn left towards the campground. Follow this road for 4.4 km (2.7 mi), passing the campground along the way. The trailhead is located on the right side of the road.

Trail Markings: None, but the trail is obvious and cannot be missed.

Trail Features: The commanding feature of this trail is the picturesque Williams Falls, which can be viewed up close from a wooden bridge and, even better, a platform a few steps farther down the trail.

Williams Falls. H.A. EISELT

BIBLIOGRAPHY

General

Chester, Q. and J. Chester. 1991. *The Outdoor Companion*. Sydney, Australia: Simon and Schuster.

Clotfelter, C.F. and M.L. Clotfelter. 1979. *Camping and Backpacking*. Detroit: Gale Research Co., Book Tower.

Craighead, G.J. 1978. *The American Walk Book*. New York: E.P. Dutton.

Elman, R. and C. Rees. 1982. *The Hiker's Bible*, Garden City: Doubleday.

Fletcher, C. 1984. *The Complete Walker III* (3rd ed.). New York: Alfred A. Knopf.

Hart, J. 1984. *Walking Softly in the Wilderness: The Sierra Club Guide to Backpacking*. San Francisco: Sierra Club Books.

Katz, E. 1980. *The Complete Guide to Backpacking in Canada*. Toronto: Doubleday.

Manning, H. 1985. *Backpacking: One Step at a Time* (4th. ed.). New York: Vintage Books.

Rethmel, R.C. 1984. *Backpacking* (7th ed.), Picataway: New Century Publishers.

Riviere, B. 1981. *The L.L. Bean Guide to the Outdoors*. New York: Random House.

Roberts, H. 1979. *Movin' Out*. Boston: Stone Wall Press.

Sandi, M. 1980. *Sports Illustrated Backpacking*. New York: J.B. Lippincott.

Waterman, L. and G. Waterman. 1979. *Backwoods Ethics: Environmental Concerns for Hikers and Campers*. Boston: Stone Wall Press.

New Brunswick

Burzynski, M. 1985. *Fundy National Park*. Vancouver: Douglas & McIntyre.

O'Donnell, K. 1993. *Heritage Trails and Footpaths on Grand Manan*. North Head: Grand Manan Tourism Association.

The Fundy Hiking Trail Association. 1988. *On Foot to Fundy*. (2nd ed.) Moncton.

Special Interest

Auerbach, P.S. 1991. *Medicine for the Outdoors*. Boston: Little, Brown and Co.

Wiseman, J. 1989. *The SAS Survival Handbook*. London: Collins Harvill.

INDEX